P9-BIW-309

AMERICAN POETS PROJECT

AMERICAN POETS PROJECT

IS PUBLISHED WITH A GIFT IN MEMORY OF

James Merrill

AND SUPPORT FROM ITS FOUNDING PATRONS

Sidney J. Weinberg, Jr. Foundation

The Berkley Foundation

Richard B. Fisher and Jeanne Donovan Fisher

# Emma Lazarus

selected poems

**john hollander** editor

AMERICAN POETS PROJECT

THE LIBRARY OF AMERICA

The paper used in this publication meets the minimum requirements of the
American National Standard for Information Sciences—Permanence of Paper
for Printed Library Materials, ANSI Z39.48—1984.

Design by Chip Kidd and Mark Melnick.
Frontispiece: Engraving by T. Johnson courtesy Library of Congress


Library of Congress Cataloging-in-Publication Data:
Lazarus, Emma, 1849–1887.
    [Poems. Selections]
    Selected poems / Emma Lazarus ; John Hollander, editor.
        p. cm. — (American poets project ; 16)
    Includes bibliographical references.
    ISBN 1–931082–77–4 (alk. paper)
      I. Hollander, John. II. Title. III. Series.

PS2233.A4H65 2005
811'.4— dc22
2004061551

10 9 8 7 6 5 4 3 2 1

Emma
Lazarus

Emma Lazarus.

# CONTENTS

# INTRODUCTION

The posthumous fame of Emma Lazarus (1849–1887) resulted from her authorship of a single poem, the sonnet whose lines are engraved on the base of the Statue of Liberty in New York harbor. It is—as is not often the case with such occasional compositions—an unusually fine poem, one of those perennial favorites (another would be Gray's "Elegy Written in a Country Church-Yard") that, almost despite their popular fame, are masterpieces of a kind. But in her lifetime Lazarus had gained recognition as a poet and person of letters while still relatively young and, despite her early death (she died of cancer at 38), produced in the latter part of her career work whose high quality (especially now that our perspective on nineteenth-century American poetry has been cleared of its last vestiges of modernist bias) has become increasingly apparent. In addition, her somewhat anomalous character as a female Jewish writer whose growing feeling for and knowledge about

Jewish identity coincided with her achievement of true poetic power adds considerably to the interest of her work.

She was born in New York City to a wealthy New York Jewish family, Sephardic on her father's side, German on her mother's; both of her grandfathers had lived in New York as far back as the American Revolution. She was educated at home, read widely, spent her summers in Newport, Rhode Island, and at quite a young age acquired a knowledge of Greek and Latin classics and modern literature in French, German, and Italian. In her lifelong devotion to verse in other languages and the importance of translation for her own poetry, Lazarus belongs to the line of American poets running from Longfellow to Pound, Robert Lowell, and W. S. Merwin. While still in her teens she translated poems by Victor Hugo, Heinrich Heine, Alexandre Dumas, and Friedrich Schiller, and she would go on to translate Petrarch, Goethe, François Coppée, Leopardi, her contemporary Giosuè Carducci, and, eventually, the great Jewish poets of medieval Spain: Judah ha-Levi, Solomon Ibn Gabirol, and Moses Ibn Ezra. She played the piano and was devoted to Chopin and Schumann, both of whom would figure in her later poetry.

According to a biographical sketch by her sister Josephine (included as the introduction to the posthumous two-volume *Poems*, a selection edited by her other sisters Mary and Annie), it was the outbreak of the Civil War that elicited the young girl's earliest verses. The poems and translations she wrote between the ages of fourteen and sixteen were published privately at her father's expense in 1866 and, with some additions, by a New York publisher the following year. They were very well received, and her literary reputation continued to grow. This first volume exhibited varying degrees of competence in verse and rhetorical force; among the few strongest are the Emersonian epigram "Links," with its fine ending, resonant because unmoralized—"And in those realms of space, all bathed in light, / Soar none except the eagle and the lark."— and the blank-verse sonnet "Niagara" and its companion piece "Niagara River Below the Falls." Imaginative ambition, only sometimes outrunning linguistic conventionality, is shown in some of the other, longer poems. Lazarus sent a copy of this volume to Ralph Waldo Emerson in 1868 and made his acquaintance at about that time. His literary friendship became crucially important for her, and they corresponded for years; when Emerson's 1874 anthology *Parnassus* appeared without a single poem of hers in it, she wrote a miffed but dignified letter of complaint. There was some reconciliation by 1876.

*Admetus and Other Poems* (1871), dedicated "To my friend, Ralph Waldo Emerson," showed major development in both poetic enterprise and technical power. Its long title poem based on the Alcestis story and the accompanying ones about Orpheus, Lohengrin, and Tannhäuser are blank-verse narratives heightened by well-wrought even if extremely Tennysonian moments. (Her later dramatic poems lean more on the influence of Browning, and "A Masque of Venice" seems to come from that poet's great "A Toccata of Galuppi's.") "Epochs," a cycle of poems on various phases of life and experience, may owe something of its structure to German *Lieder* cycles; its epigraph from Emerson points to an understanding of the successive poems not as the mere record of moments in the young woman's life, but as a series of major tropes, whose poetic consequences she was beginning to explore. By 1872, her poetry was appearing frequently in *Lippincott's Magazine*, as it would for the next eight years. She published a romantic novel, *Alide* (1874), based on an episode in the life of Goethe—Turgenev wrote of it admiringly to her, perhaps over-admiringly—and a verse drama, *The Spagnoletto* (1876).

Many of the most striking of Lazarus' earlier poems use music as a point of departure. The sequence of four sonnets called "Chopin" starts out with a record of attentive and informed listening to a Chopin waltz, but moves into a refiguring of Chopin as Orpheus—as musician-poet speaking not only for romanticism and for Poland, but as "A voice for all whom Fate hath set apart, / Who, still misprized, must perish by the way. . . ." Lazarus' fascination with Schumann surfaced in her 1874 "Phantasies" in terzarima, written as poetic responses to Schumann's *Phantasiestücke*, op. 12, and even translating the titles of the pieces in Schumann's suite. The following year she published "Scenes in the Wood," in which each of the sections corresponds to one of the parts of his *Waldszenen*, op. 82. The culmination of her involvement with Schumann is "Symphonic Studies" (1878), a suite of eight sonnets inspired by *Symphonische Etuden*, op. 13, one theme followed by twelve etudes—no programmatic correspondence here, but instead the introduction of a Prospero-like figure who renders "harmless" a tempest in the "Prelude," followed by a sea-poem and then by a capriccio of figures of life and love and sorrow: and, over all, the poem is structured by the poet's personal master-trope of working through a series.

The free flow of images in some of these poems of the 1870s sets Lazarus apart from most of her contemporaries. The beautiful catalogue of remembered impressions in "Long Island Sound," for example, is grandly free of the sort of prosy explaining and pointing of morals that, in the work of Longfellow and others, pads and weakens so much American verse of the nineteenth century:

      . . . the sparkle far and wide,
Laughter of unseen children, cheerful chirp
Of crickets, and low lisp of rippling tide,
Light summer clouds fantastical as sleep
Changing unnoted while I gazed thereon.
All these fair sounds and sights I made my own.

Her pivotal sonnet of 1880 called "Echoes"—beginning "Late-born and woman-souled I dare not hope, / The freshness of the elder lays, the might / Of manly, modern passion shall alight / Upon my Muse's lips"—represents something of a turning point in her sense of her poetic career. The poem confronts a later—not an early—sense of belatedness at a point when she had already started to overcome it in practice. It is as if she has only just become aware of how good she might get to be—as if, after initial success, only doubts could confirm true vocation. And even though she had been engaging history and issues of social and political protest in her poems, it is as if, after about the age of thirty, she came to find the easy exposition of some of the historically topical verse she had written quite inadequate.

It is notable that the early poem "The Jewish Synagogue at Newport" (1867), a response to Longfellow's celebrated poem about the cemetery there, might easily have been written by a Gentile poet with a bit of knowledge of post-biblical Jewish history, and seems written from outside the diasporic condition of exile. In later years Lazarus would undoubtedly have treated this subject very differently. Lazarus' sister Josephine implied in her biographical essay that it was not until 1881 that Lazarus began to concern herself with Judaic matters in her poetry and essays. This was not, however, a sudden awakening. Her poetry had tentatively addressed her Jewish identity for some years, and by 1877 she had begun to translate medieval Hebrew poetry from German versions; she started to study the language itself five years later. The depth of her imaginative engagement with the poetry of Heinrich Heine, whom she felt to be a major precursor both as a Jew and a romantic ironist, was made clear by the book of Heine translations that she published in 1881, which included excellent versions of the long cycles *Die Heimkehr* and the free-verse *Die Nordsee*.

It was also in 1881 that she became acutely aware of the pogroms occurring in Russia, and she personally witnessed the exilic arrival in the United States of Eastern European Jewish refugees. The following year, she published a piece of strong polemic in *The Century* against a defender of the Russian peasant mobs. Her 1882 collection *Songs of a Semite: The Dance to Death and Other Poems* (included in Volume II of the 1889 *Poems*) contained work of greater power and imaginative scope than anything she had previously published. Even if some of these poems occasionally fell into an exhortatory mode something like Whittier's, in others she achieved a tone of ironic prophetic vehemence, and with "In Exile" she reached major lyrical depth.

The growing intensity of her study of Jewish history and culture led her to try to write poems that could deal with Judaic matters while remaining American in mode and tone and stance. In a passage from one of her essays on post-biblical Jewish history and culture published under the title "Epistle to the Hebrews," Lazarus propounded an interesting little allegory on a point of grammar—the *pi'el*, or intensive form of the Hebrew verb:

> "Every student of the Hebrew language is aware that we have in the conjugation of our verbs a mode known as the intensive voice, which, by means of an

almost imperceptible modification of vowel points, intensifies the meaning of the primitive root. A similar significance seems to attach to the Jews themselves in connection with the people among whom they dwell. They are the intensive form of any nationality whose language and customs they adopt."

Here Lazarus seems to be thinking at once of German Jewry (and, as always, Heine), and how American Jewish culture might play an analogous role in America. She seems also to be thinking, by extension, of what role she might play as a poet and an educated American woman.

Before Lazarus, the only Jewish poets in the United States were the humorist Bret Harte and the little-known Penina Moise (1797–1880), who was born and lived and wrote in Charleston, South Carolina. Moise was the author of a volume called *Fancy's Sketch Book* (1833), as well as a collection of hymns for the reformed Jewish congregation of that city. Many of her verses speak of, and for, the South, but one of them, "To Persecuted Foreigners," addresses a matter that seems to foreshadow a later period in American history. In its third stanza, she invokes one group of these in particular:

> If thou art one of that oppressed race,
> Whose pilgrimage from Palestine we trace,
> Brave the Atlantic—Hope's broad anchor weigh,
> A Western Sun will gild your future day.

Jewish immigration at this point in the nineteenth century would largely have been from German-speaking territories, rather than composed of the Eastern European "wretched refuse" of "The New Colossus," Emma Lazarus' much more powerful, beautiful, and consequential poem. The "we" in Moise's lines speaks for enlightened American historical knowledge, rather than Jewish or Jewish-American identity. But in any event none of Lazarus' few Jewish precursors was a poet of her gifts and stature, and none of them in their lives or work struggled, as she did, with major problems of modernity and American poetics.

After the publication of *Songs of a Semite*, Lazarus published a good many prose pieces—some on literature and drama, but most of them on the historical and political plight of the Jews—and fewer poems. She traveled abroad in France and England—where she met Robert Browning, who befriended her, and William Morris, whom she greatly admired—in 1883. The following year she fell ill with an undiagnosed illness that left her drained of energy. After her father's death in 1885, she again went abroad, hoping to recover from her own illness, and was deeply impressed by her first encounter with Italy. In England and France during the following year her illness, apparently a malignancy, worsened, and after returning to the United States in the summer of 1887, she died on November 17.

Except as the author of "The New Colossus," her name sank into obscurity after the publication of the posthumous *Poems*, and an attempt to collect and publish a volume of her complete poetry in 1926 was effectively blocked by her sister Annie, who held the rights; by this time an Anglo-Catholic convert, she forbade the reprinting of anything of Judaic concern in her sister's work. Nonetheless Lazarus' reputation has grown steadily over the last sixty years, and one can hope for further critical revaluation.

"The New Colossus" was written in 1883, after her return from her first European trip, as part of a fundraiser for the cost of a pedestal for Frédéric Auguste Bartholdi's colossal statue (braced from within by a structure designed by Eiffel) of "Liberty Enlightening the World." (Lazarus had initially rejected the commission, apparently reluctant to write "on order.") In its title the poem immediately confronts the huge scale of the statue (Bartholdi apparently often claimed that the statue's huge size was "in keeping with the magnitude of the idea"). But the poem also works with the statue's probably unwitting allusion to a gigantic precursor placed in another harbor: the Colossus of Rhodes, one of the Seven Wonders of the (Hellenistic) World, a statue of Helios, god of the sun, that guarded a busy and important harbor. Lazarus reads Bartholdi's torch-bearing *Liberté* as a revisionary and antithetical figure: female, welcoming rather than minatory, with a broken shackle at her feet, and holding a version of one of the Tablets of the Law, inscribed with the date July 4, 1776. What we might call her meta-colossal size, her scale, is one of greatness rather than grossness. And, from the very first line of Lazarus' beautifully wrought sonnet, Liberty's bronze is compared to the literal and figurative brass of the Rhodian figure's composition and attitude.

Lazarus refigures the heavily literal straddling of the Colossus (it was a common error to believe that the ancient Colossus straddled the harbor entrance) in the image of Liberty's gaze in which she bridges the twin cities, New York and Brooklyn—"air-bridged" although the Brooklyn Bridge had opened the previous May. Her torch is "the imprisoned lightning," able (as in Shelley's sonnet "England in 1819") to illuminate but not to destroy, and replacing the "flaming sword" of the guardian angel in Genesis.

The fine construction of this sonnet—the ecphrastic description in the octave followed by the notional speech ("with silent lips") of the statue in the sestet; the balanced placement of the broken lines 6 and 10, the way the whole poem gives resonance to the final line—exemplifies how well Emma Lazarus came to write in this form.

The sonnet "1492," written shortly before "The New

Colossus," seems to lay the ground for the Liberty poem, most pointedly in the unrevised figure of the flaming sword of Genesis 3:23, "which turned every way," forever to block the return to Paradise, but also more generally in the mythopoetic space it opens. The year that Americans associate with the voyage of Columbus and the discovery of America can be no simple moment of epochal dawn for the poet Lazarus had become. For an American Jew, it is Janus-faced, a threshold year through which time brings at once hope and despair, profit and loss, redemption and wretchedness, all in the time of the expulsion of the Jews from Spain. Lazarus sees these two events as somehow intertwined; the order in which she presents them, in the backward-gazing octave and the forward-looking sestet, urges a Providential reading, and the Columbian prospect is taken as negating the European and possibly even re-deeming the time:

> Then smiling, thou unveil'dst, O two-faced year,
> A virgin world where doors of sunset part,
> Saying, "Ho, all who weary, enter here!
> There falls each ancient barrier that the art
> Of race or creed or rank devised, to rear
> Grim bulwarked hatred between heart and heart!"

The "all who weary, enter here!" does not use the word "hope," but nevertheless deliberately invokes in re-versal the Dantean inscription over the gate of Hell: "Abandon all hope, you who enter here." The redemptive American promise of "1492" contrasts strongly with the purely negative sense of that year in another poem Lazarus wrote on the same theme: "The Exodus (August 3, 1492)," the first of her powerful and original suite of prose poems "By the Waters of Babylon," written in the same month.

"The New Colossus" and "1492" are only two of

Lazarus' many fine sonnets. What Wordsworth called "the sonnet's scanty plot of ground" granted her greater concision in her early work, and, as she continued to develop her craft, a greater concentration of imaginative energy. She began promisingly with the blank-verse sonnet "Niagara" and the untitled one, from her second book, on Mount Katahdin ("Still northward is the central mount of Maine"), a poem that perhaps reflects an awareness of Emerson's "Monadnoc," but that also engages the agenda of Bryant's injunction to the painter Thomas Cole leaving for Europe to "keep that wilder image bright": "Our noble scenes have yet no history. / All subtler charms than those that feed the eye / Our lives must give them." Another notable sonnet, which has never been precisely dated, is the manuscript poem "Assurance," not published until recently, an erotic reverie somewhat redolent of Dante Gabriel Rossetti that has invited speculation about the more obscure regions of Lazarus' personal life.

In the nineteenth century, female writers were hardly neglected (Hawthorne is said to have contemplated writing under a female pseudonym to better his chances at publication). But among the consequences of twentieth-century high modernism's popularity was a process of historical canonization, in which aesthetic distinction became a central matter (and in which romantic tradition, in Britain and America, was undervalued). While Emily Dickinson's greatness was acknowledged (interestingly, she was sometimes considered a proto-modernist), twentieth-century feminist backlash initiated a spirited revision, not only of the canon, but of canonicity itself. This enterprise came up with a great many female poets neglected since 1914, and deserving, it was claimed, of the greatest attention, but often in an intellectual venue in which relative poetic strength and imaginative power seemed to be treated as intrusive shadows from a now disqualified realm of discourse. But Emma Lazarus' work in the last fifteen years of her life acquired a depth of aesthetic seriousness and mode of poetic originality of a peculiar sort for her century. (Only the work of Sarah Piatt, a very good poet, shares some of the ironic bite of Lazarus' later poems.)

Her exploration of what the cultural position of an American Jewish writer (regardless of gender) might be prefigured modernism's more general concern with American poetic identity, and a postmodern focus on what used to be called hyphenated ethnicities. The concerns she voiced in her literary and cultural essays came increasingly to be reflected in her poems, of which the language continued to grow stronger and more compact, the diction more pointed, and the tone more complex. Had she lived another twenty years, these developments might have led to work that the modernist taste of fifty years ago could have found of great interest. But the work as it stands is most impressive, and Emma Lazarus' position in nineteenth-century American poetry remains unique.

*John Hollander*
*2004*

## Niagara

Thou art a giant altar, where the Earth
Must needs send up her thanks to Him above
Who did create her. Nature cometh here
To lay its offerings upon thy shrine.
The morning and the evening shower down
Bright jewels,—changeful opals, em'ralds fair.
The burning noon sends floods of molten gold,
The calm night crowns thee with its host of stars,
The moon enfolds thee with her silver veil,
And o'er thee e'er is arched the rainbow's span,—
The gorgeous marriage-ring of Earth and Heaven.
While ever from the holy altar grand
Ascends the incense of the mist and spray,
That mounts to God with thy wild roar of praise.

CLIFTON HOUSE, NIAGARA FALLS, CANADA,
  *August 24th, 1865.*

## Niagara River Below the Falls

Flow on forever, in thy tranquil sleep,
Thou stream, all wearied by thy giant leap;
Flow on in quiet and in peace fore'er,
No rocky steep, no precipice is there.

The rush, the roar, the agony are past;
The leap, the mighty fall, are o'er at last;
And now with drowsy ripplings dost thou flow,
All murmuring in whispers soft and low.

Oh tell us, slumb'ring, em'rald river, now,
With that torn veil of foam upon thy brow;
Now, while thou sleepest quietly below,—
What are thy dreams? Spent river, let us know.

Again, in thought, dost dash o'er that dread steep.
By frenzy maddened to the fearful leap?
By passion's mists all blinded, cold and white,
Dost plunge once more, now, from the dizzy height?

Or else, forgetful of the dangers past,
Art dreaming calm and peacefully, at last,
Of that fair nymph who pressed thy livid brow,
And gave thy past a glory vanished now?

The *Rainbow*, whom the royal Sun e'er wooes,
For whom, in tears, the mighty Storm-king sues;
Who left her cloud-built palace-home above,
To crown thy awful brow with light and love.

Yes, in thy tranquil sleep, O wearied stream,
Still of the lovely Iris is thy dream;
The agony, the perils ne'er could last;
But with all these the rainbow, too, has past.

No life so wild and hopeless but some gleam
Doth lighten it, to make a future dream.
Thy course, O Stream, has been mid fears and woe,
But thou hast met the Rainbow in thy flow.

NEW YORK, *November 3d, 1865.*

## Florence Nightingale

Upon the whitewashed walls
A woman's shadow falls,
A woman walketh o'er the darksome floors.
A soft, angelic smile
Lighteth her face the while,
In passing through the dismal corridors.

And now and then there slips
A word from out her lips,
More sweet and grateful to those listening ears
Than the most plaintive tale
Of the sad nightingale,
Whose name and tenderness this woman bears.

Her presence in the room
Of agony and gloom,
No fretful murmurs, no coarse words profane;
For while she standeth there,
All words are hushed save prayer;
She seems God's angel weeping o'er man's pain.

And some of them arise,
With eager, tearful eyes,
From off their couch to see her passing by.

Some, e'en too weak for this,
    Can only stoop and kiss
Her shadow, and fall back content to die.

    No monument of stone
    Needs this heroic one,—
Her name is graven on each noble heart;
    And in all after years
    Her praise will be the tears
Which at that name from quivering lids will start.

    And those who live not now,
    To see the sainted brow,
And the angelic smile before it flits for aye,
    They in the future age
    Will kiss the storied page
Whereon the shadow of her life will lie.

*March 7, 1867.*

## Dreams

A dream of lilies: all the blooming earth,
    A garden full of fairies and of flowers;
Its only music the glad cry of mirth,
    While the warm sun weaves golden-tissued hours;
Hope a bright angel, beautiful and true
    As Truth herself, and life a lovely toy,
Which ne'er will weary us, ne'er break, a new
    Eternal source of pleasure and of joy.

A dream of roses: vision of Love's tree,
    Of beauty and of madness, and as bright
As naught on earth save only dreams can be,
    Made fair and odorous with flower and light;
A dream that Love is strong to outlast Time,
    That hearts are stronger than forgetfulness,
The slippery sand than changeful waves that climb,
    The wind-blown foam than mighty waters' stress.

A dream of laurels: after much is gone,
    Much buried, much lamented, much forgot,
With what remains to do and what is done,
    With what yet is, and what, alas! is not,
Man dreams a dream of laurel and of bays,
    A dream of crowns and guerdons and rewards,
Wherein sounds sweet the hollow voice of praise,
    And bright appears the wreath that it awards.

A dream of poppies, sad and true as Truth,—
    That all these dreams were dreams of vanity;
And full of bitter penitence and ruth,
    In his last dream, man deems 'twere good to die;
And weeping o'er the visions vain of yore,
    In the sad vigils he doth nightly keep,
He dreams it may be good to dream no more,
    And life has nothing like Death's dreamless sleep.

*April 30, 1867.*

## On a Tuft of Grass

Weak, slender blades of tender green,
With little fragrance, little sheen,
    What maketh ye so dear to all?
Nor bud, nor flower, nor fruit have ye,
So tiny, it can only be
    'Mongst fairies ye are counted tall.

No beauty is in this,—ah, yea,
E'en as I gaze on you to-day,
    Your hue and fragrance bear me back
Into the green, wide fields of old,
With clear, blue air, and manifold
    Bright buds and flowers in blossoming track.

All bent one way like flickering flame,
Each blade caught sunlight as it came,
    Then rising, saddened into shade;
A changeful, wavy, harmless sea,
Whose billows none could bitterly
    Reproach with wrecks that they had made.

No gold ever was buried there
More rich, more precious, or more fair
    Than buttercups with yellow gloss.
No ships of mighty forest trees
E'er foundered in these guiltless seas
    Of grassy waves and tender moss.

Ah, no! ah, no! not guiltless still,
Green waves on meadow and on hill,
    Not wholly innocent are ye;
For what dead hopes and loves, what graves,
Lie underneath your placid waves,
    While breezes kiss them lovingly!

Calm sleepers with sealed eyes lie there;
They see not, neither feel nor care
    If over them the grass be green.
And some sleep here who ne'er knew rest,
Until the grass grew o'er their breast,
    And stilled the aching pain within.

Not all the sorrow man hath known,
Not all the evil he hath done,
    Have ever cast thereon a stain.
It groweth green and fresh and light,
As in the olden garden bright,
    Beneath the feet of Eve and Cain.

It flutters, bows, and bends, and quivers,
And creeps through forests and by rivers,
    Each blade with dewy brightness wet,
So soft, so quiet, and so fair,
We almost dream of sleeping there,
    Without or sorrow or regret.

*May 22, 1867.*

# In the Jewish Synagogue at Newport

Here, where the noises of the busy town,
  The ocean's plunge and roar can enter not,
We stand and gaze around with tearful awe,
  And muse upon the consecrated spot.

No signs of life are here: the very prayers
  Inscribed around are in a language dead;
The light of the "perpetual lamp" is spent
  That an undying radiance was to shed.

What prayers were in this temple offered up,
  Wrung from sad hearts that knew no joy on earth,
By these lone exiles of a thousand years,
  From the fair sunrise land that gave them birth!

Now as we gaze, in this new world of light,
  Upon this relic of the days of old,
The present vanishes, and tropic bloom
  And Eastern towns and temples we behold.

Again we see the patriarch with his flocks,
  The purple seas, the hot blue sky o'erhead,
The slaves of Egypt,—omens, mysteries,—
  Dark fleeing hosts by flaming angels led.

A wondrous light upon a sky-kissed mount,
  A man who reads Jehovah's written law,
'Midst blinding glory and effulgence rare,
  Unto a people prone with reverent awe.

The pride of luxury's barbaric pomp,
   In the rich court of royal Solomon—
Alas! we wake: one scene alone remains,—
   The exiles by the streams of Babylon.

Our softened voices send us back again
   But mournful echoes through the empty hall;
Our footsteps have a strange unnatural sound,
   And with unwonted gentleness they fall.

The weary ones, the sad, the suffering,
   All found their comfort in the holy place,
And children's gladness and men's gratitude
   Took voice and mingled in the chant of praise.

The funeral and the marriage, now, alas!
   We know not which is sadder to recall;
For youth and happiness have followed age,
   And green grass lieth gently over all.

Nathless the sacred shrine is holy yet,
   With its lone floors where reverent feet once trod.
Take off your shoes as by the burning bush,
   Before the mystery of death and God.

*July, 1867.*

# In a Swedish Graveyard

"They all sleep with their heads to the westward. Each held a lighted taper in his hand when he died; and in his coffin were placed his little heart-treasures and a piece of money for his last journey."

LONGFELLOW, *Rural Life in Sweden.*

After wearisome toil and much sorrow,
    How quietly sleep they at last,
Neither dreading and fearing the morrow,
    Nor vainly bemoaning the past!
Shall we give them our envy or pity?
    Shall we shun or yearn after such rest,
So calm near the turbulent city,
    With their heart stilled at length in their breast?

They all sleep with their heads lying westward,
    Where all suns and all days have gone down.
Do they long for the dawn, looking eastward?
    Do they dream of the strife and the crown?
Each one held a lit taper when dying:
    Where hath vanished the fugitive flame?
With his love, and his joy, and his sighing,
    Alas! and his youth and his name.

The living stands o'er him and dreameth,
    And wonders what dreams came to him.
While the tender, brief twilight still gleameth,
    With a light strangely mournful and dim.
And he wonders what lights and what shadows
    Passed over these dead long ago,

When their feet now at rest trod these meadows,
  And their hearts throbbed to pleasure or woe.

What dreams came to them in their living?
  The self-same that come now to thee.
If thou findest those dreams are deceiving,
  Then these lives thou wilt know and wilt see:
The same visions of love and of glory,
  The same vain regret for the past;
All the same poor and pitiful story,
  Till the taper's extinguished at last.

All the treasures on earth that they cherished,
  Now they care not to clasp nor to save;
And the poor little lights, how they perished,
  Slowly dying alone in the grave!
With a flickering faint on the features
  Of age, or of youth in its bloom:
Lighting up for grim Death his weak creatures,
  In the darkness and night of the tomb,—

With a radiance ghostly and mournful,
  On the good, on the just and unjust;
For a space, till the monarch, so scornful,
  Turned the light and the lighted to dust.
No taper of earth he desired
  In his halls where they quietly rest;
For all those who have toiled and are tired,
  Utter darkness and sleep may be best.

*1867.*

## The Garden of Adonis

*(The Garden of Life in Spenser's "Faerie Queene.")*

It is no fabled garden in the skies,
　　But bloometh here,—this is no world of death;
And nothing that once liveth, ever dies,
And naught that breathes can ever cease to breathe,
　　And naught that bloometh ever withereth.
The gods can ne'er take back their gifts from men,
They gave us life,—they cannot take again.

Who hath known Death, and who hath seen his face?
　　On what high mountain have ye met with him?
Within what lowest valley is there trace
　　Of his feared footsteps? in what forest dim,
In what great city, in what lonely ways?
Nay, there is no such god, but one called Change,
And all he does is beautiful and strange.

It is but Change that lays our darlings low,
　　And, though we doubt and fear, forsakes them not.
Where red lips smiled do sweetest roses blow,
　　And star-flowers bloom above the lovely spot
　　Where gleamed the eyes, with blue forget-me-not.
And through the grasses runs the same wave there
We knew of old within the golden hair.

Dig in the earth,—ye shall not surely find
　　Death or death's semblance; only roots of flowers,
And all fair, goodly things there live enshrined,
　　With the foundations of the glad green bowers,

Through which the sunshine comes in golden
      showers.
And all the blossoms that this earth enwreathe,
Are for assurance that there is no death.

O mother, raise thy tear-bathed lids again:
   Thy child died not, he only liveth more,—
His soul is in the sunshine and the rain,
   His life is in the waters and the shore,
   He is around thee all the wide world o'er;
The daisy thou hast plucked smiles back at thee,
Because it doth again its mother see.

What noble deed that ever lived, is dead,
   Or yet hath lost its power to inspire
Courage in hearts that sicken, and to shed
   New faith and hope when hands and footsteps tire,
   And make sad, downcast eyes look upward higher?
Yea, all men see and know it, whence it came;
It purifies them like a burning flame.

And dreams? What dreams were ever lost and gone,
   But wandering in strange lands we found again?
When least we think of these dear birdlings flown,
   We find that bright and fresh they still remain.
   The garden of all life is round us then;
And he is blind who doth not know and see,
And praise the gods for immortality.

*May, 1868.*

# Morning

Gray-vested Dawn, with flameless, tranquil eye,
Cool hands, and dewy lips, is in the sky,
A sober nun, with starry rosary.

With eyes downcast and with uplifted palm,
She seems to whisper now her silent psalm;
Beneath her gaze the sleeping earth is calm.

Her prayer is ended, and she riseth slow,
And o'er the hills she quietly doth go,
Noiseless and gentle as the midnight snow.

Then suddenly the pale east blushes red,
The flowers to see upraise a sleepy head,
The rosy colors deepen, grow, and spread.

A cool breeze whispers: "She is coming now!"
And then the radiant colors burn and glow,
The white east blushes over cheek and brow,

And glorious on the hills the Morning stands,
Her saffron hair back-blown from rosy bands,
And light and joy and fragrance in her hands.

Her foot has touched the hill-tops, and they shine;
She comes,—the willow rustles and the pine;
She smiles upon the fields a smile divine,

And all the earth smiles back; from mount to vale,
From oak to shuddering grass, from glen to dale,
Wet fields and flowers and glistening brooks cry "Hail!"


## Exultation

Behold, I walked abroad at early morning,
The fields of June were bathed in dew and lustre,
The hills were clad with light as with a garment.

The inexpressible auroral freshness,
The grave, immutable, aerial heavens,
The transient clouds above the quiet landscape,

The heavy odor of the passionate lilacs,
That hedged the road with sober-colored clusters,
All these o'ermastered me with subtle power,

And made my rural walk a royal progress,
Peopled my solitude with airy spirits,
Who hovered over me with joyous singing.

"Behold!" they sang, "the glory of the morning.
Through every vein does not the summer tingle,
With vague desire and flush of expectation?

"To think how fair is life! set round with grandeur;
The eloquent sea beneath the voiceless heavens,
The shifting shows of every bounteous season;

"Rich skies, fantastic clouds, and herby meadows,
Gray rivers, prairies spread with regal flowers,
Grasses and grains and herds of browsing cattle:

"Great cities filled with breathing men and women,
Of whom the basest have their aspirations,
High impulses of courage or affection.

"And on this brave earth still those finer spirits,
Heroic Valor, admirable Friendship,
And Love itself, a very god among you.

"All these for thee, and thou evoked from nothing,
Born from blank darkness to this blaze of beauty,
Where is thy faith, and where are thy thanksgivings?"

The world is his who can behold it rightly,
Who hears the harmonies of unseen angels
Above the senseless outcry of the hour.


## Sonnet

Still northward is the central mount of Maine,
    From whose high crown the rugged forests seem
    Like shaven lawns, and lakes with frequent gleam,
"Like broken mirrors," flash back light again.
Eastward the sea, with its majestic plain,
Endless, of radiant, restless blue, superb
With might and music, whether storms perturb

Its reckless waves, or halcyon winds that reign,
Make it serene as wisdom. Storied Spain
   Is the next coast, and yet we may not sigh
For lands beyond the inexorable main;
   Our noble scenes have yet no history.
   All subtler charms than those that feed the eye,
Our lives must give them; 'tis an aim austere,
But opes new vistas, and a pathway clear.


## The Day of Dead Soldiers
*May 30, 1869*


Welcome, thou gray and fragrant Sabbath-day,
   To deathless love and valor dedicate!
Glorious with the richest flowers of May,
   With early roses, lingering lilacs late,
With vivid green of grass and leaf and spray,
Thou bringest memories that far outweigh
   The season's joy with thoughts of death and fate.

What words may paint the picture on the air
   Of this broad land to-day from sea to sea?
The rolling prairies, purple valleys rare,
   And royal mountains, endless rivers free,
Filled full with phantoms flitting everywhere,
Pale ghosts of buried armies, slowly there
   From countless graves uprising silently.

A calm, grave day,—the sunlight does not shine,
  But thin, gray clouds bedrape the sky o'erhead.
The delicate air is filled with spirits fine,
  The temperate breezes whisper of the dead.
What visions and what memories divine,
O holy Sabbath flower-day, are thine,
  Painted in light against a field of red!

Behold the fairest spots in all the land,
  To-day in this mid-season of fresh flowers,
Are heroes' graves,—by many a tender hand
  Sprinkled with odorous, radiant-colored showers;
By mild, moist breezes delicately fanned,
Sending o'er distant towns their perfumes bland,
  Loading with sweet aroma sunless hours.

Who knows what tremulous, dusky hands set free,
  Deck quaintly with gay flowers the graves unknown?
What wealth of bloom is shed exuberantly,
  On the far grave in Illinois alone,
Where the last hero, sleeping peacefully,
Beyond detraction and mistrust, doth lie,
  By the glad winds of prairies overblown?

With hymns and prayer be this day sanctified,
  And consecrate to heroes' memories;
Not with wild, violent grief for those who died,
  O wives and mothers, but with patience wise,
Calm resignation, and a thankful pride,
That they have left their land a fame so wide,
  So rich a page of thrilling histories.

FROM
## Epochs

*"The epochs of our life are not in the visible facts, but in the silent thought by the wayside as we walk."*—EMERSON.

### I. Youth

Sweet empty sky of June without a stain,
   Faint, gray-blue dewy mists on far-off hills,
Warm, yellow sunlight flooding mead and plain,
   That each dark copse and hollow overfills;
   The rippling laugh of unseen, rain-fed rills,
Weeds delicate-flowered, white and pink and gold,
A murmur and a singing manifold.

The gray, austere old earth renews her youth
   With dew-lines, sunshine, gossamer, and haze.
How still she lies and dreams, and veils the truth,
   While all is fresh as in the early days!
   What simple things be these the soul to raise
To bounding joy, and make young pulses beat,
With nameless pleasure finding life so sweet.

On such a golden morning forth there floats,
   Between the soft earth and the softer sky,

In the warm air adust with glistening motes,
    The mystic winged and flickering butterfly,
    A human soul, that hovers giddily
Among the gardens of earth's paradise,
Nor dreams of fairer fields or loftier skies.

## II. Regret

Thin summer rain on grass and bush and hedge,
    Reddening the road and deepening the green
On wide, blurred lawn, and in close-tangled sedge;
    Veiling in gray the landscape stretched between
    These low broad meadows and the pale hills seen
But dimly on the far horizon's edge.

In these transparent-clouded, gentle skies,
    Wherethrough the moist beams of the soft June sun
Might any moment break, no sorrow lies,
    No note of grief in swollen brooks that run,
    No hint of woe in this subdued, calm tone
Of all the prospect unto dreamy eyes.

Only a tender, unnamed half-regret
    For the lost beauty of the gracious morn;
A yearning aspiration, fainter yet,
    For brighter suns in joyous days unborn,
    Now while brief showers ruffle grass and corn,
And all the earth lies shadowed, grave, and wet;

Space for the happy soul to pause again
    From pure content of all unbroken bliss,

To dream the future void of grief and pain,
    And muse upon the past, in reveries
    More sweet for knowledge that the present is
Not all complete, with mist and clouds and rain.

*    *    *

### IV. Storm

Serene was morning with clear, winnowed air,
    But threatening soon the low, blue mass of cloud
Rose in the west, with mutterings faint and rare
    At first, but waxing frequent and more loud.
    Thick sultry mists the distant hill-tops shroud;
The sunshine dies; athwart black skies of lead
Flash noiselessly thin threads of lightning red.

Breathless the earth seems waiting some wild blow,
    Dreaded, but far too close to ward or shun.
Scared birds aloft fly aimless, and below
    Naught stirs in fields whence light and life are gone,
    Save floating leaves, with wisps of straw and down,
Upon the heavy air; 'neath blue-black skies,
Livid and yellow the green landscape lies.

And all the while the dreadful thunder breaks,
    Within the hollow circle of the hills,
With gathering might, that angry echoes wakes,
    And earth and heaven with unused clamor fills.
    O'erhead still flame those strange electric thrills.
A moment more,—behold! yon bolt struck home,
And over ruined fields the storm hath come!

## How Long?

How long, and yet how long,
Our leaders will we hail from over seas,
Masters and kings from feudal monarchies,
    And mock their ancient song
With echoes weak of foreign melodies?

That distant isle mist-wreathed,
Mantled in unimaginable green,
Too long hath been our mistress and our queen.
    Our fathers have bequeathed
Too deep a love for her, our hearts within.

She made the whole world ring
With the brave exploits of her children strong,
And with the matchless music of her song.
    Too late, too late we cling
To alien legends, and their strains prolong.

This fresh young world I see,
With heroes, cities, legends of her own;
With a new race of men, and overblown
    By winds from sea to sea,
Decked with the majesty of every zone.

I see the glittering tops
Of snow-peaked mounts, the wid'ning vale's expanse,
Large prairies where free herds of horses prance,
    Exhaustless wealth of crops,
In vast, magnificent extravagance.

These grand, exuberant plains,
These stately rivers, each with many a mouth,
The exquisite beauty of the soft-aired south,
    The boundless seas of grains,
Luxuriant forests' lush and splendid growth.

    The distant siren-song
Of the green island in the eastern sea,
Is not the lay for this new chivalry.
    It is not free and strong
To chant on prairies 'neath this brilliant sky.

    The echo faints and fails;
It suiteth not, upon this western plain,
Our voice or spirit; we should stir again
    The wilderness, and make the vales
Resound unto a yet unheard-of strain.


## Heroes

    In rich Virginian woods,
The scarlet creeper reddens over graves,
Among the solemn trees enlooped with vines;
Heroic spirits haunt the solitudes,—
The noble souls of half a million braves,
    Amid the murmurous pines.

    Ah! who is left behind,
Earnest and eloquent, sincere and strong,
To consecrate their memories with words

Not all unmeet? with fitting dirge and song
To chant a requiem purer than the wind,
    And sweeter than the birds?

    Here, though all seems at peace,
The placid, measureless sky serenely fair,
The laughter of the breeze among the leaves,
The bars of sunlight slanting through the trees,
The reckless wild-flowers blooming everywhere,
    The grasses' delicate sheaves,—

    Nathless each breeze that blows,
Each tree that trembles to its leafy head
With nervous life, revives within our mind,
Tender as flowers of May, the thoughts of those
Who lie beneath the living beauty, dead,—
    Beneath the sunshine, blind.

    For brave dead soldiers, these:
Blessings and tears of aching thankfulness,
Soft flowers for the graves in wreaths enwove,
The odorous lilac of dear memories,
The heroic blossoms of the wilderness,
    And the rich rose of love.

    But who has sung their praise,
Not less illustrious, who are living yet?
Armies of heroes, satisfied to pass
Calmly, serenely from the whole world's gaze,
And cheerfully accept, without regret,
    Their old life as it was,

With all its petty pain,
Its irritating littleness and care;
They who have scaled the mountain, with content
Sublime, descend to live upon the plain;
Steadfast as though they breathed the mountain-air
   Still, wheresoe'er they went.


 They who were brave to act,
And rich enough their action to forget;
Who, having filled their day with chivalry,
Withdraw and keep their simpleness intact,
And all unconscious add more lustre yet
   Unto their victory.


On the broad Western plains
Their patriarchal life they live anew;
Hunters as mighty as the men of old,
Or harvesting the plenteous, yellow grains,
Gathering ripe vintage of dusk bunches blue,
   Or working mines of gold;


Or toiling in the town,
Armed against hindrance, weariness, defeat,
With dauntless purpose not to swerve or yield,
And calm, defiant strength, they struggle on,
As sturdy and as valiant in the street,
   As in the camp and field.


And those condemned to live,
Maimed, helpless, lingering still through suffering years,
May they not envy now the restful sleep

Of the dear fellow-martyrs they survive?
Not o'er the dead, but over these, your tears,
 O brothers, ye may weep!

 New England fields I see,
The lovely, cultured landscape, waving grain,
Wide, haughty rivers, and pale, English skies.
And lo! a farmer ploughing busily,
Who lifts a swart face, looks upon the plain,—
 I see, in his frank eyes,

 The hero's soul appear.
Thus in the common fields and streets they stand;
The light that on the past and distant gleams,
They cast upon the present and the near,
With antique virtues from some mystic land,
 Of knightly deeds and dreams.

## Links

The little and the great are joined in one
By God's great force. The wondrous golden sun
Is linked unto the glow-worm's tiny spark;
The eagle soars to heaven in his flight;
And in those realms of space, all bathed in light,
Soar none except the eagle and the lark.

## Phantasies

(*After Robert Schumann*)

### I. Evening

Rest, beauty, stillness: not a waif of cloud
From gray-blue east sheer to the yellow west—
No film of mist the utmost slopes to shroud.

The earth lies grave, by quiet airs caressed,
And shepherdeth her shadows, but each stream,
Free to the sky, is by that glow possessed,

And traileth with the splendors of a dream
Athwart the dusky land. Uplift thine eyes!
Unbroken by a vapor or a gleam,

The vast clear reach of mild, wan twilight skies.
But look again, and lo, the evening star!
Against the pale tints black the slim elms rise,

The earth exhales sweet odors nigh and far,
And from the heavens fine influences fall.
Familiar things stand not for what they are:

What they suggest, foreshadow, or recall
The spirit is alert to apprehend,
Imparting somewhat of herself to all.

Labor and thought and care are at an end:
The soul is filled with gracious reveries,
And with her mood soft sounds and colors blend;

For simplest sounds ring forth like melodies
In this weird-lighted air—the monotone
Of some far bell, the distant farmyard cries,

A barking dog, the thin, persistent drone
Of crickets, and the lessening call of birds.
The apparition of yon star alone

Breaks on the sense like music. Beyond words
The peace that floods the soul, for night is here,
And Beauty still is guide and harbinger.


## II. *Aspiration*

Dark lies the earth, and bright with worlds the sky:
That soft, large, lustrous star, that first outshone,
Still holds us spelled with potent sorcery.

Dilating, shrinking, lightening, it hath won
Our spirit with its strange strong influence,
And sways it as the tides beneath the moon.

What impulse this, o'ermastering heart and sense?
Exalted, thrilled, the freed soul fain would soar
Unto that point of shining prominence,

Craving new fields and some unheard-of shore,
Yea, all the heavens, for her activity,
To mount with daring flight, to hover o'er

Low hills of earth, flat meadows, level sea,
And earthly joy and trouble. In this hour
Of waning light and sound, of mystery,

Of shadowed love and beauty-veilèd power,
She feels her wings: she yearns to grasp her own,
Knowing the utmost good to be her dower.

A dream! a dream! for at a touch 't is gone.
O mocking spirit! thy mere fools are we,
Unto the depths from heights celestial thrown.

From these blind gropings toward reality,
This thirst for truth, this most pathetic need
Of something to uplift, to justify,

To help and comfort while we faint and bleed,
May we not draw, wrung from the last despair,
Some argument of hope, some blessed creed,

That we can trust the faith which whispers prayer,
The vanishings, the ecstasy, the gleam,
The nameless aspiration, and the dream?


*III. Wherefore?*

Deep languor overcometh mind and frame:
A listless, drowsy, utter weariness,
A trance wherein no thought finds speech or name,

The overstrainèd spirit doth possess.
She sinks with drooping wing—poor unfledged bird,
That fain had flown!—in fluttering breathlessness.

To what end those high hopes that wildly stirred
The beating heart with aspirations vain?
Why proffer prayers unanswered and unheard

To blank, deaf heavens that will not heed her pain?
Where lead these lofty, soaring tendencies,
That leap and fly and poise, to fall again,

Yet seem to link her with the utmost skies?
What mean these clinging loves that bind to earth,
And claim her with beseeching, wistful eyes?

This little resting-place 'twixt death and birth,
Why is it fretted with the ceaseless flow
Of flood and ebb, with overgrowth and dearth,

And vext with dreams, and clouded with strange woe?
Ah! she is tired of thought, she yearns for peace,
Seeing all things one equal end must know.

Wherefore this tangle of perplexities,
The trouble or the joy? the weary maze
Of narrow fears and hopes that may not cease?

A chill falls on her from the skyey ways,
Black with the night-tide, where is none to hear
The ancient cry, the Wherefore of our days.

## IV. Fancies

The ceaseless whirr of crickets fills the ear
From underneath each hedge and bush and tree,
Deep in the dew-drenched grasses everywhere.

The simple sound dispels the fantasy
Of gloom and terror gathering round the mind.
It seems a pleasant thing to breathe, to be,

To hear the many-voiced, soft summer wind
Lisp through the dark thick leafage overhead—
To see the rosy half-moon soar behind

The black slim-branching elms. Sad thoughts have fled,
Trouble and doubt, and now strange reveries
And odd caprices fill us in their stead.

From yonder broken disk the redness dies,
Like gold fruit through the leaves the half-sphere
    gleams,
Then over the hoar tree-tops climbs the skies,

Blanched ever more and more, until it beams
Whiter than crystal. Like a scroll unfurled,
And shadowy as a landscape seen in dreams,

Reveals itself the sleeping, quiet world,
Painted in tender grays and whites subdued—
The speckled stream with flakes of light impearled,

The wide, soft meadow and the massive wood.
Naught is too wild for our credulity
In this weird hour: our finest dreams hold good.

Quaint elves and frolic flower-sprites we see,
And fairies weaving rings of gossamer,
And angels floating through the filmy air.

### V. In the Night

Let us go in: the air is dank and chill
With dewy midnight, and the moon rides high
O'er ghostly fields, pale stream, and spectral hill.

This hour the dawn seems farthest from the sky
So weary long the space that lies between
That sacred joy and this dark mystery

Of earth and heaven: no glimmering is seen,
In the star-sprinkled east, of coming day,
Nor, westward, of the splendor that hath been.

Strange fears beset us, nameless terrors sway
The brooding soul, that hungers for her rest,
Outworn with changing moods, vain hopes' delay,

With conscious thought o'erburdened and oppressed.
The mystery and the shadow wax too deep;
She longs to merge both sense and thought in sleep.

## VI. Faerie

From the oped lattice glance once more abroad
While the ethereal moontide bathes with light
Hill, stream, and garden, and white-winding road.

All gracious myths born of the shadowy night
Recur, and hover in fantastic guise,
Airy and vague, before the drowsy sight.

On yonder soft gray hill Endymion lies
In rosy slumber, and the moonlit air
Breathes kisses on his cheeks and lips and eyes.

'Twixt bush and bush gleam flower-white limbs, left
    bare,
Of huntress-nymphs, and flying raiment thin,
Vanishing faces, and bright floating hair.

The quaint midsummer fairies and their kin,
Gnomes, elves, and trolls, on blossom, branch, and grass
Gambol and dance, and winding out and in

Leave circles of spun dew where'er they pass.
Through the blue ether the freed Ariel flies;
Enchantment holds the air; a swarming mass

Of myriad dusky, gold-winged dreams arise,
Throng toward the gates of sense, and so possess
The soul, and lull it to forgetfulness.

## VII. *Confused Dreams*

O strange, dim other-world revealed to us,
Beginning there where ends reality,
Lying 'twixt life and death, and populous

With souls from either sphere! now enter we
Thy twisted paths. Barred is the silver gate,
But the wild-carven doors of ivory

Spring noiselessly apart: between them straight
Flies forth a cloud of nameless shadowy things,
With harpies, imps, and monsters, small and great,

Blurring the thick air with their darkening wings.
All humors of the blood and brain take shape,
And fright us with our own imaginings.

A trouble weighs upon us: no escape
From this unnatural region can there be.
Fixed eyes stare on us, wide mouths grin and gape,

Familiar faces out of reach we see.
Fain would we scream, to shatter with a cry
The tangled woof of hideous fantasy,

When, lo! the air grows clear, a soft fair sky
Shines overhead: sharp pain dissolves in peace;
Beneath the silver archway quietly

We float away: all troublous visions cease.
By a strange sense of joy we are possessed,
Body and spirit soothed in perfect rest.

### VIII. The End of the Song

What dainty note of long-drawn melody
Athwart our dreamless sleep rings sweet and clear,
Till all the fumes of slumber are brushed by,

And with awakened consciousness we hear
The pipe of birds? Look forth! The sane, white day
Blesses the hilltops, and the sun is near.

All misty phantoms slowly roll away
With the night's vapors toward the western sky.
The Real enchants us, the fresh breath of hay

Blows toward us; soft the meadow-grasses lie,
Bearded with dew; the air is a caress;
The sudden sun o'ertops the boundary

Of eastern hills, the morning joyousness
Thrills tingling through the frame; life's pulse beats
    strong;
Night's fancies melt like dew. So ends the song!

## Arabesque

On a background of pale gold
I would trace with quaint design,
    Penciled fine,
Brilliant-colored, Moorish scenes,
Mosques and crescents, pages, queens,
    Line on line,
That the prose-world of to-day
Might the gorgeous Past's array
    Once behold.

On the magic painted shield
Rich Granada's *Vega* green
    Should be seen;
Crystal fountains, coolness flinging,
Hanging gardens' skyward springing
    Emerald sheen;
Ruddy when the daylight falls,
Crowned Alhambra's beetling walls
    Stand revealed;

Balconies that overbrow
Field and city, vale and stream.
    In a dream
Lulled the drowsy landscape basks;
Weary toilers cease their tasks.
    Mark the gleam
Silvery of each white-swathed peak!
Mountain-airs caress the cheek,
    Fresh from snow.

Here in Lindaraxa's bower
The immortal roses bloom;
	In the room
Lion-guarded, marble-paven,
Still the fountain leaps to heaven.
	But the doom
Of the banned and stricken race
Overshadows every place,
	Every hour.

Where fair Lindaraxa dwelt
Flits the bat on velvet wings;
	Mute the strings
Of the broken mandoline;
The Pavilion of the Queen
	Widely flings
Vacant windows to the night;
Moonbeams kiss the floor with light
	Where she knelt.

Through these halls that people stepped
Who through darkling centuries
	Held the keys
Of all wisdom, truth, and art,
In a Paradise apart,
	Lapped in ease,
Sagely pondering deathless themes,
While, befooled with monkish dreams,
	Europe slept.

Where shall they be found to-day?
Yonder hill that frets the sky
    "The Last Sigh
Of the Moor" is namèd still.
There the ill-starred Boabdil
    Bade good-by
To Granada and to Spain,
Where the Crescent ne'er again
    Holdeth sway.

Vanished like the wind that blows,
Whither shall we seek their trace
    On earth's face?
The gigantic wheel of fate,
Crushing all things soon or late,
    Now a race,
Now a single life o'erruns,
Now a universe of suns,
    Now a rose.

## Off Rough Point

We sat at twilight nigh the sea,
  The fog hung gray and weird.
Through the thick film uncannily
  The broken moon appeared.

We heard the billows crack and plunge,
  We saw nor waves nor ships.

Earth sucked the vapors like a sponge,
  The salt spray wet our lips.

Closer the woof of white mist drew,
  Before, behind, beside.
How could that phantom moon break through,
  Above that shrouded tide?

The roaring waters filled the ear,
  A white blank foiled the sight.
Close-gathering shadows near, more near,
  Brought the blind, awful night.

O friends who passed unseen, unknown!
  O dashing, troubled sea!
Still stand we on a rock alone,
  Walled round by mystery.

## Fog

Light silken curtain, colorless and soft,
Dreamlike before me floating! what abides
        Behind thy pearly veil's
        Opaque, mysterious woof?

Where sleek red kine, and dappled, crunch day-long
Thick, luscious blades and purple clover-heads,
        Nigh me I still can mark
        Cool fields of beaded grass.

No more; for on the rim of the globed world
I seem to stand and stare at nothingness.
        But songs of unseen birds
        And tranquil roll of waves

Bring sweet assurance of continuous life
Beyond this silvery cloud. Fantastic dreams,
        Of tissue subtler still
        Than the wreathed fog, arise,

And cheat my brain with airy vanishings
And mystic glories of the world beyond.
        A whole enchanted town
        Thy baffling folds conceal—

An Orient town, with slender-steepled mosques,
Turret from turret springing, dome from dome,
        Fretted with burning stones,
        And trellised with red gold.

Through spacious streets, where running waters flow,
Sun-screened by fruit-trees and the broad-leaved palm,
        Past the gay-decked bazaars,
        Walk turbaned, dark-eyed men.

Hark! you can hear the many murmuring tongues,
While loud the merchants vaunt their gorgeous wares.
        The sultry air is spiced
        With fragrance of rich gums,

And through the lattice high in yon dead wall,
See where, unveiled, an arch, young, dimpled face,
      Flushed like a musky peach,
      Peers down upon the mart!

From her dark, ringleted and bird-poised head
She hath cast back the milk-white silken veil:
      'Midst the blank blackness there
      She blossoms like a rose.

Beckons she not with those bright, full-orbed eyes,
And open arms that like twin moonbeams gleam?
      Behold her smile on me
      With honeyed, scarlet lips!

Divine Scheherazade! I am thine.
I come! I come!—Hark! from some far-off mosque
      The shrill muezzin calls
      The hour of silent prayer,

And from the lattice he hath scared my love.
The lattice vanisheth itself—the street,
      The mart, the Orient town;
      Only through still, soft air

That cry is yet prolonged. I wake to hear
The distant fog-horn peal: before mine eyes
      Stands the white wall of mist,
      Blending with vaporous skies.

Elusive gossamer, impervious
Even to the mighty sun-god's keen red shafts!

With what a jealous art
Thy secret thou dost guard!

Well do I know deep in thine inmost folds,
Within an opal hollow, there abides
        The lady of the mist,
        The Undine of the air—

A slender, winged, ethereal, lily form,
Dove-eyed, with fair, free-floating, pearl-wreathed hair,
        In waving raiment swathed
        Of changing, irised hues.

Where her feet, rosy as a shell, have grazed
The freshened grass, a richer emerald glows:
        Into each flower-cup
        Her cool dews she distills.

She knows the tops of jagged mountain-peaks,
She knows the green soft hollows of their sides,
        And unafraid she floats
        O'er the vast-circled seas.

She loves to bask within the moon's wan beams,
Lying, night-long upon the moist, dark earth,
        And leave her seeded pearls
        With morning on the grass.

Ah! that athwart these dim, gray outer courts
Of her fantastic palace I might pass,
        And reach the inmost shrine
        Of her chaste solitude,

And feel her cool and dewy fingers press
My mortal-fevered brow, while in my heart
  She poured with tender love
  Her healing Lethe-balm!

See! the close curtain moves, the spell dissolves!
Slowly it lifts: the dazzling sunshine streams
  Upon a newborn world
  And laughing summer seas.

Swift, snowy-breasted sandbirds twittering glance
Through crystal air. On the horizon's marge,
  Like a huge purple wraith,
  The dusky fog retreats.


## Song

*Venus*

Frosty lies the winter-landscape,
  In the twilight golden-green.
Down the Park's deserted alleys,
  Naked elms stand stark and lean.

Dumb the murmur of the fountain,
  Birds have flown from lawn and hill.
But while yonder star's ascendant,
  Love triumphal reigneth still.

See the keen flame throb and tremble,
   Brightening in the darkening night,
Breathing like a thing of passion,
   In the sky's smooth chrysolite.

Not beneath the moon, oh lover,
   Thou shalt gain thy heart's desire.
Speak to-night! The gods are with thee
   Burning with a kindred fire.


## The South

Night, and beneath star-blazoned summer skies
   Behold the Spirit of the musky South,
A creole with still-burning, languid eyes,
   Voluptuous limbs and incense-breathing mouth:
      Swathed in spun gauze is she,
From fibres of her own anana tree.

Within these sumptuous woods she lies at ease,
   By rich night-breezes, dewy cool, caressed:
'Twixt cypresses and slim palmetto trees,
   Like to the golden oriole's hanging nest,
      Her airy hammock swings,
And through the dark her mocking-bird yet sings.

How beautiful she is! A tulip-wreath
   Twines round her shadowy, free-floating hair:
Young, weary, passionate, and sad as death,

Dark visions haunt for her the vacant air,
　　　　While movelessly she lies
With lithe, lax, folded hands and heavy eyes.

Full well knows she how wide and fair extend
　　Her groves bright-flowered, her tangled everglades,
Majestic streams that indolently wend
　　Through lush savanna or dense forest shades,
　　　　Where the brown buzzard flies
To broad bayous 'neath hazy-golden skies.

Hers is the savage splendor of the swamp,
　　With pomp of scarlet and of purple bloom,
Where blow warm, furtive breezes faint and damp,
　　Strange insects whir, and stalking bitterns boom—
　　　　Where from stale waters dead
Oft looms the great-jawed alligator's head.

Her wealth, her beauty, and the blight on these,—
　　Of all she is aware: luxuriant woods,
Fresh, living, sunlit, in her dream she sees;
　　And ever midst those verdant solitudes
　　　　The soldier's wooden cross,
O'ergrown by creeping tendrils and rank moss.

Was hers a dream of empire? was it sin?
　　And is it well that all was borne in vain?
She knows no more than one who slow doth win,
　　After fierce fever, conscious life again,
　　　　Too tired, too weak, too sad,
By the new light to be or stirred or glad.

From rich sea-islands fringing her green shore,
From broad plantations where swart freemen bend
Bronzed backs in willing labor, from her store
Of golden fruit, from stream, from town, ascend
Life-currents of pure health:
Her aims shall be subserved with boundless wealth.

Yet now how listless and how still she lies,
Like some half-savage, dusky Indian queen,
Rocked in her hammock 'neath her native skies,
With the pathetic, passive, broken mien
Of one who, sorely proved,
Great-souled, hath suffered much and much hath loved!

But look! along the wide-branched, dewy glade
Glimmers the dawn: the light palmetto-trees
And cypresses reissue from the shade,
And *she* hath wakened. Through clear air she sees
The pledge, the brightening ray,
And leaps from dreams to hail the coming day.

## Magnetism

By the impulse of my will,
By the red flame in my blood,
By my nerves' electric thrill,
By the passion of my mood,
My concentrated desire,
My undying, desperate love,

I ignore Fate, I defy her,
  Iron-hearted Death I move.
When the town lies numb with sleep,
  Here, round-eyed I sit; my breath
Quickly stirred, my flesh a-creep,
  And I force the gates of death.
I nor move nor speak—you'd deem
  From my quiet face and hands,
I were tranced—but in her dream,
  *She* responds, she understands.
I have power on what is not,
  Or on what has ceased to be,
From that deep, earth-hollowed spot,
  I can lift her up to me.
And, or ere I am aware
  Through the closed and curtained door,
Comes my lady white and fair,
  And embraces me once more.
Though the clay clings to her gown,
  Yet all heaven is in her eyes;
Cool, kind fingers press mine eyes,
  To my soul her soul replies.
But when breaks the common dawn,
  And the city wakes—behold!
My shy phantom is withdrawn,
  And I shiver lone and cold.
And I know when she has left,
  She is stronger far than I,
And more subtly spun her weft,
  Than my human wizardry.
Though I force her to my will,
  By the red flame in my blood,

By my nerves' electric thrill,
   By the passion of my mood,
Yet all day a ghost am I.
   Nerves unstrung, spent will, dull brain.
I achieve, attain, but die,
   And she claims me hers again.


## August Moon

Look! the round-cheeked moon floats high,
In the glowing August sky,
Quenching all her neighbor stars,
Save the steady flame of Mars.
White as silver shines the sea,
Far-off sails like phantoms be,
Gliding o'er that lake of light,
Vanishing in nether night.
Heavy hangs the tasseled corn,
Sighing for the cordial morn;
But the marshy-meadows bare,
Love this spectral-lighted air,
Drink the dews and lift their song,
Chirp of crickets all night long;
Earth and sea enchanted lie
'Neath that moon-usurped sky.

To the faces of our friends
Unfamiliar traits she lends—
Quaint, white witch, who looketh down
With a glamour all her own.

Hushed are laughter, jest, and speech,
Mute and heedless each of each,
In the glory wan we sit,
Visions vague before us flit;
Side by side, yet worlds apart,
Heart becometh strange to heart.

Slowly in a moved voice, then,
Ralph, the artist, spake again—
"Does not that weird orb unroll
Scenes phantasmal to your soul?
As I gaze thereon, I swear,
Peopled grows the vacant air,
Fables, myths alone are real,
White-clad sylph-like figures steal
'Twixt the bushes, o'er the lawn,
Goddess, nymph, undine, and faun.
Yonder, see the *Willis* dance,
Faces pale with stony glance;
They are maids who died unwed,
And they quit their gloomy bed,
Hungry still for human pleasure,
Here to trip a moonlit measure.
Near the shore the mermaids play,
Floating on the cool, white spray,
Leaping from the glittering surf
To the dark and fragrant turf,
Where the frolic trolls, and elves
Daintily disport themselves.
All the shapes by poet's brain,
Fashioned, live for me again,

In this spiritual light,
Less than day, yet more than night.
What a world! a waking dream,
All things other than they seem,
Borrowing a finer grace,
From yon golden globe in space;
Touched with wild, romantic glory,
Foliage fresh and billows hoary,
Hollows bathed in yellow haze,
Hills distinct and fields of maize,
Ancient legends come to mind.
Who would marvel should he find,
In the copse or nigh the spring,
Summer fairies gamboling
Where the honey-bees do suck,
Mab and Ariel and Puck?
Ah! no modern mortal sees
Creatures delicate as these.
All the simple faith has gone
Which their world was builded on.
Now the moonbeams coldly glance
On no gardens of romance;
To prosaic senses dull,
Baldur's dead, the Beautiful,
Hark, the cry rings overhead,
'Universal Pan is dead!'"
"*Requiescant!*" Claude's grave tone
Thrilled us strangely. "I am one
Who would not restore that Past,
Beauty will immortal last,
Though the beautiful must die—

This the ages verify.
And had Pan deserved the name
Which his votaries misclaim,
He were living with us yet.
I behold, without regret,
Beauty in new forms recast,
Truth emerging from the vast,
Bright and orbed, like yonder sphere,
Making the obscure air clear.
He shall be of bards the king,
Who, in worthy verse, shall sing
All the conquests of the hour,
Stealing no fictitious power
From the classic types outworn,
But his rhythmic line adorn
With the marvels of the real.
He the baseless feud shall heal
That estrangeth wide apart
Science from her sister Art.
Hold! look through this glass for me?
Artist, tell me what you see?"
"I!" cried Ralph. "I see in place
Of Astarte's silver face,
Or veiled Isis' radiant robe,
Nothing but a rugged globe
Seamed with awful rents and scars.
And below no longer Mars,
Fierce, flame-crested god of war,
But a lurid, flickering star,
Fashioned like our mother earth,
Vexed, belike, with death and birth."

Rapt in dreamy thought the while,
With a sphinx-like shadowy smile,
Poet Florio sat, but now
Spake in deep-voiced accents slow,
More as one who probes his mind,
Than for us—"Who seeks, shall find—
Widening knowledge surely brings
Vaster themes to him who sings.
Was veiled Isis more sublime
Than yon frozen fruit of Time,
Hanging in the naked sky?
Death's domain—for worlds too die.
Lo! the heavens like a scroll
Stand revealed before my soul;
And the hieroglyphs are suns—
Changeless change the law that runs
Through the flame-inscribed page,
World on world and age on age,
Balls of ice and orbs of fire,
What abides when these expire?
Through slow cycles they revolve,
Yet at last like clouds dissolve.
Jove, Osiris, Brahma pass,
Races wither like the grass.
Must not mortals be as gods
To embrace such periods?
Yet at Nature's heart remains
One who waxes not nor wanes.
And our crowning glory still
Is to have conceived his will."

## A Masque of Venice
(*A Dream*)

Not a stain,
In the sun-brimmed sapphire cup that is the sky—
Not a ripple on the black translucent lane
Of the palace-walled lagoon.
Not a cry
As the gondoliers with velvet oar glide by,
Through the golden afternoon.

From this height
Where the carved, age-yellowed balcony o'erjuts
Yonder liquid, marble pavement, see the light
Shimmer soft beneath the bridge
That abuts
On a labyrinth of water-ways and shuts
Half their sky off with its ridge.

We shall mark
All the pageant from this ivory porch of ours,
Masques and jesters, mimes and minstrels, while
  we hark
To their music as they fare.
Scent their flowers
Flung from boat to boat in rainbow radiant showers
Through the laughter-ringing air.

See! they come,
Like a flock of serpent-throated black-plumed swans,
With the mandoline, the viol, and the drum,

Gems afire on arms ungloved,
           Fluttering fans,
Floating mantles like a great moth's streaky vans
Such as Veronese loved.

           But behold
In their midst a white unruffled swan appear.
One strange barge that snowy tapestries enfold,
White its tasseled, silver prow.
           Who is here?
Prince of Love in masquerade or Prince of Fear,
Clad in glittering silken snow?

           Cheek and chin
Where the mask's edge stops are of the hoar-frost's hue,
And no eyebeams seem to sparkle from within
Where the hollow rings have place.
           Yon gay crew
Seem to fly him, he seems ever to pursue.
'T is our sport to watch the race.

           At his side
Stands the goldenest of beauties; from her glance,
From her forehead, shines the splendor of a bride,
And her feet seem shod with wings
           To entrance,
For she leaps into a wild and rhythmic dance,
Like Salome at the King's.

　　　　　　'T is his aim
Just to hold, to clasp her once against his breast,
Hers to flee him, to elude him in the game.
Ah, she fears him overmuch!
　　　　　　Is it jest,—
Is it earnest? a strange riddle lurks half-guessed
In her horror of his touch.


　　　　　　For each time
That his snow-white fingers reach her, fades some ray
From the glory of her beauty in its prime;
And the knowledge grows upon us that the dance
　　　　　　Is no play
'Twixt the pale, mysterious lover and the fay—
But the whirl of fate and chance.


　　　　　　Where the tide
Of the broad lagoon sinks plumb into the sea,
There the mystic gondolier hath won his bride.
Hark, one helpless, stifled scream!
　　　　　　Must it be?
Mimes and minstrels, flowers and music, where are ye?
Was all Venice such a dream?

## SONNETS

### Echoes

Late-born and woman-souled I dare not hope,
The freshness of the elder lays, the might
Of manly, modern passion shall alight
Upon my Muse's lips, nor may I cope
(Who veiled and screened by womanhood must grope)
With the world's strong-armed warriors and recite
The dangers, wounds, and triumphs of the fight;
Twanging the full-stringed lyre through all its scope.
But if thou ever in some lake-floored cave
O'erbrowed by rocks, a wild voice wooed and heard,
Answering at once from heaven and earth and wave,
Lending elf-music to thy harshest word,
Misprize thou not these echoes that belong
To one in love with solitude and song.

### Success

Oft have I brooded on defeat and pain,
The pathos of the stupid, stumbling throng.
These I ignore to-day and only long
To pour my soul forth in one trumpet strain,
One clear, grief-shattering, triumphant song,
For all the victories of man's high endeavor,
Palm-bearing, laureled deeds that live forever,

The splendor clothing him whose will is strong.
Hast thou beheld the deep, glad eyes of one
Who has persisted and achieved? Rejoice!
On naught diviner shines the all-seeing sun.
Salute him with free heart and choral voice,
'Midst flippant, feeble crowds of spectres wan,
The bold, significant, successful man.


## The New Colossus*

Not like the brazen giant of Greek fame,
With conquering limbs astride from land to land;
Here at our sea-washed, sunset gates shall stand
A mighty woman with a torch, whose flame
Is the imprisoned lightning, and her name
Mother of Exiles. From her beacon-hand
Glows world-wide welcome; her mild eyes command
The air-bridged harbor that twin cities frame.
"Keep, ancient lands, your storied pomp!" cries she
With silent lips. "Give me your tired, your poor,
Your huddled masses yearning to breathe free,
The wretched refuse of your teeming shore.
Send these, the homeless, tempest-tost to me,
I lift my lamp beside the golden door!"

*Written in aid of Bartholdi Pedestal Fund, 1883.

## Venus of the Louvre

Down the long hall she glistens like a star,
The foam-born mother of Love, transfixed to stone,
Yet none the less immortal, breathing on.
Time's brutal hand hath maimed but could not mar.
When first the enthralled enchantress from afar
Dazzled mine eyes, I saw not her alone,
Serenely poised on her world-worshipped throne,
As when she guided once her dove-drawn car,—
But at her feet a pale, death-stricken Jew,
Her life adorer, sobbed farewell to love.
Here *Heine* wept! Here still he weeps anew,
Nor ever shall his shadow lift or move,
While mourns one ardent heart, one poet-brain,
For vanished Hellas and Hebraic pain.

## Chopin

I.

A dream of interlinking hands, of feet
Tireless to spin the unseen, fairy woof,
Of the entangling waltz. Bright eyebeams meet,
Gay laughter echoes from the vaulted roof.
Warm perfumes rise; the soft unflickering glow
Of branching lights sets off the changeful charms
Of glancing gems, rich stuffs, the dazzling snow
Of necks unkerchieft, and bare, clinging arms.
Hark to the music! How beneath the strain

Of reckless revelry, vibrates and sobs
One fundamental chord of constant pain,
The pulse-beat of the poet's heart that throbs.
So yearns, though all the dancing waves rejoice,
The troubled sea's disconsolate, deep voice.

## II.

Who shall proclaim the golden fable false
Of Orpheus' miracles?  This subtle strain
Above our prose-world's sordid loss and gain
Lightly uplifts us. With the rhythmic waltz,
The lyric prelude, the nocturnal song
Of love and languor, varied visions rise,
That melt and blend to our enchanted eyes.
The Polish poet who sleeps silenced long,
The seraph-souled musician, breathes again
Eternal eloquence, immortal pain.
Revived the exalted face we know so well,
The illuminated eyes, the fragile frame,
Slowly consuming with its inward flame,
We stir not, speak not, lest we break the spell.

## III.

A voice was needed, sweet and true and fine
As the sad spirit of the evening breeze,
Throbbing with human passion, yet divine
As the wild bird's untutored melodies.
A voice for him 'neath twilight heavens dim,
Who mourneth for his dead, while round him fall
The wan and noiseless leaves. A voice for him
Who sees the first green sprout, who hears the call

Of the first robin on the first spring day.
A voice for all whom Fate hath set apart,
Who, still misprized, must perish by the way,
Longing with love, for that they lack the art
Of their own soul's expression. For all these
Sing the unspoken hope, the vague, sad reveries.

### IV.

Then Nature shaped a poet's heart—a lyre
From out whose chords the lightest breeze that blows
Drew trembling music, wakening sweet desire.
How shall she cherish him? Behold! she throws
This precious, fragile treasure in the whirl
Of seething passions; he is scourged and stung,
Must dive in storm-vext seas, if but one pearl
Of art or beauty therefrom may be wrung.
No pure-browed pensive nymph his Muse shall be,
An amazon of thought with sovereign eyes,
Whose kiss was poison, man-brained, worldly-wise,
Inspired that elfin, delicate harmony.
Rich gain for us! But with him is it well?
The poet who must sound earth, heaven, and hell!

## Symphonic Studies

*(After Robert Schumann.)*

### PRELUDE

Blue storm-clouds in hot heavens of mid-July
    Hung heavy, brooding over land and sea:

Our hearts, a-tremble, throbbed in harmony
With the wild, restless tone of air and sky.
Shall we not call him Prospero who held
    In his enchanted hands the fateful key
    Of that tempestuous hour's mystery,
And with controlling wand our spirits spelled,
With him to wander by a sun-bright shore,
    To hear fine, fairy voices, and to fly
With disembodied Ariel once more
    Above earth's wrack and ruin? Far and nigh
The laughter of the thunder echoed loud,
And harmless lightnings leapt from cloud to cloud.


I.

Floating upon a swelling wave of sound,
    We seemed to overlook an endless sea:
    Poised 'twixt clear heavens and glittering surf
            were we.
We drank the air in flight: we knew no bound
To the audacious ventures of desire.
    Nigh us the sun was dropping, drowned in gold;
    Deep, deep below the burning billows rolled;
And all the sea sang like a smitten lyre.
Oh, the wild voices of those chanting waves!
    The human faces glimpsed beneath the tide!
Familiar eyes gazed from profound sea-caves,
    And we, exalted, were as we had died.
We knew the sea was Life, the harmonious cry
The blended discords of humanity.

II.

Look deeper yet: mark 'midst the wave-blurred mass,
  In lines distinct, in colors clear defined,
  The typic groups and figures of mankind.
Behold within the cool and liquid glass
Bright child-folk sporting with smooth yellow shells,
  Astride of dolphins, leaping up to kiss
  Fair mother-faces. From the vast abyss
How joyously their thought-free laughter wells!
Some slumber in grim caverns unafraid,
  Lulled by the overwhelming water's sound,
And some make mouths at dragons, undismayed.
  Oh dauntless innocence! The gulfs profound
Reëcho strangely with their ringing glee,
And with wise mermaids' plaintive melody.


III.

What do the sea-nymphs in that coral cave?
  With wondering eyes their supple forms they bend
  O'er something rarely beautiful. They lend
Their lithe white arms, and through the golden wave
They lift it tenderly. Oh blinding sight!
  A naked, radiant goddess, tranced in sleep,
  Full-limbed, voluptuous, 'neath the mantling sweep
Of auburn locks that kiss her ankles white!
Upward they bear her, chanting low and sweet:
  The clinging waters part before their way,
Jewels of flame are dancing 'neath their feet.
  Up in the sunshine, on soft foam, they lay
Their precious burden, and return forlorn.
Oh, bliss! oh, anguish! Mortals, *Love* is born!

Hark! from unfathomable deeps a dirge
   Swells sobbing through the melancholy air:
   Where Love has entered, Death is also there.
The wail outrings the chafed, tumultuous surge;
Ocean and earth, the illimitable skies,
   Prolong one note, a mourning for the dead,
   The cry of souls not to be comforted.
What piercing music! Funeral visions rise,
And send the hot tears raining down our cheek.
   We see the silent grave upon the hill
   With its lone lilac-bush. O heart, be still!
She will not rise, she will not stir nor speak.
Surely, the unreturning dead are blest.
Ring on, sweet dirge, and knell us to our rest!

V.

Upon the silver beach the undines dance
   With interlinking arms and flying hair;
   Like polished marble gleam their limbs left bare;
Upon their virgin rites pale moonbeams glance.
Softer the music! for their foam-bright feet
   Print not the moist floor where they trip their round:
   Affrighted they will scatter at a sound,
Leap in their cool sea-chambers, nimbly fleet,
And we shall doubt that we have ever seen,
   While our sane eyes behold stray wreaths of mist,
   Shot with faint colors by the moon-rays kissed,
Floating snow-soft, snow-white, where these had been.
Already, look! the wave-washed sands are bare,
And mocking laughter ripples through the air.

Divided 'twixt the dream-world and the real,
    We heard the waxing passion of the song
    Soar as to scale the heavens on pinions strong.
Amidst the long-reverberant thunder-peal,
Against the rain-blurred square of light, the head
    Of the pale poet at the lyric keys
    Stood boldly cut, absorbed in reveries,
While over it keen-bladed lightnings played.
"Rage on, wild storm!" the music seemed to sing:
    "Not all the thunders of thy wrath can move
The soul that's dedicate to worshipping
    Eternal Beauty, everlasting Love."
No more! the song was ended, and behold,
A rainbow trembling on a sky of gold!


EPILOGUE

Forth in the sunlit, rain-bathed air we stepped,
    Sweet with the dripping grass and flowering vine,
    And saw through irised clouds the pale sun shine.
Back o'er the hills the rain-mist slowly crept
Like a transparent curtain's silvery sheen;
    And fronting us the painted bow was arched,
    Whereunder the majestic cloud-shapes marched:
In the wet, yellow light the dazzling green
Of lawn and bush and tree seemed stained with blue.
    Our hearts o'erflowed with peace. With smiles we
        spake
Of partings in the past, of courage new,
    Of high achievement, of the dreams that make
A wonder and a glory of our days,
And all life's music but a hymn of praise.

## Long Island Sound

I see it as it looked one afternoon
In August,—by a fresh soft breeze o'erblown.
The swiftness of the tide, the light thereon,
A far-off sail, white as a crescent moon.
The shining waters with pale currents strewn,
The quiet fishing-smacks, the Eastern cove,
The semi-circle of its dark, green grove.
The luminous grasses, and the merry sun
In the grave sky; the sparkle far and wide,
Laughter of unseen children, cheerful chirp
Of crickets, and low lisp of rippling tide,
Light summer clouds fantastical as sleep
Changing unnoted while I gazed thereon.
And these fair sounds and sights I made my own.


## Destiny

*1856*

Paris, from throats of iron, silver, brass,
Joy-thundering cannon, blent with chiming bells,
And martial strains, the full-voiced pæan swells.
The air is starred with flags, the chanted mass
Throngs all the churches, yet the broad streets swarm
With glad-eyed groups who chatter, laugh, and pass,
In holiday confusion, class with class.
And over all the spring, the sun-floods warm!
In the Imperial palace that March morn,

The beautiful young mother lay and smiled;
For by her side just breathed the Prince, her child,
Heir to an empire, to the purple born,
Crowned with the Titan's name that stirs the heart
Like a blown clarion—one more Bonaparte.

*1879*

Born to the purple, lying stark and dead,
Transfixed with poisoned spears, beneath the sun
Of brazen Africa! Thy grave is one,
Fore-fated youth (on whom were visited
Follies and sins not thine), whereat the world,
Heartless howe'er it be, will pause to sing
A dirge, to breathe a sigh, a wreath to fling
Of rosemary and rue with bay-leaves curled.
Enmeshed in toils ambitious, not thine own,
Immortal, loved boy-Prince, thou tak'st thy stand
With early doomed Don Carlos, hand in hand
With mild-browed Arthur, Geoffrey's murdered son.
Louis the Dauphin lifts his thorn-ringed head,
And welcomes thee, his brother, 'mongst the dead.

## From One Augur to Another

So, Calchas, on the sacred Palatine,
You thought of Mopsus, and o'er wastes of sea
A flower brought your message. I divine
(Through my deep art) the kindly mockery
That played about your lips and in your eyes,

Plucking the frail leaf, while you dreamed of home.
Thanks for the silent greeting! I shall prize,
Beyond June's rose, the scentless flower of Rome.
All the Campagna spreads before my sight,
The mouldering wall, the Cæsars' tombs unwreathed,
Rome and the Tiber, and the yellow light,
Wherein the honey-colored blossom breathed.
But most I thank it—egoists that we be!
For proving then and there you thought of me.


## The Cranes of Ibycus

There was a man who watched the river flow
Past the huge town, one gray November day.
Round him in narrow high-piled streets at play
The boys made merry as they saw him go,
Murmuring half-loud, with eyes upon the stream,
The immortal screed he held within his hand.
For he was walking in an April land
With Faust and Helen. Shadowy as a dream
Was the prose-world, the river and the town.
Wild joy possessed him; through enchanted skies
He saw the cranes of Ibycus swoop down.
He closed the page, he lifted up his eyes,
Lo—a black line of birds in wavering thread
Bore him the greetings of the deathless dead!

## Critic and Poet

*An Apologue*

("Poetry must be simple, sensuous, or impassioned;
this man is neither simple, sensuous, nor impassioned;
therefore he is not a poet.")

No man had ever heard a nightingale,
When once a keen-eyed naturalist was stirred
To study and define—*what is a bird*,
To classify by rote and book, nor fail
To mark its structure and to note the scale
Whereon its song might possibly be heard.
Thus far, no farther;—so he spake the word.
When of a sudden,—hark, the nightingale!

Oh deeper, higher than he could divine
That all-unearthly, untaught strain! He saw
The plain, brown warbler, unabashed. "Not mine"
(He cried) "the error of this fatal flaw.
No bird is this, it soars beyond my line,
Were it a bird, 't would answer to my law."

## St. Michael's Chapel

When the vexed hubbub of our world of gain
Roars round about me as I walk the street,
The myriad noise of Traffic, and the beat
Of Toil's incessant hammer, the fierce strain
Of Struggle hand to hand and brain to brain,

Ofttimes a sudden dream my sense will cheat,
The gaudy shops, the sky-piled roofs retreat,
And all at once I stand enthralled again
Within a marble minster over-seas.
I watch the solemn gold-stained gloom that creeps
To kiss an alabaster tomb, where sleeps
A lady 'twixt two knights' stone effigies,
And every day in dusky glory steeps
Their sculptured slumber of five centuries.


## Life and Art

Not while the fever of the blood is strong,
The heart throbs loud, the eyes are veiled, no less
With passion than with tears, the Muse shall bless
The poet-soul to help and soothe with song.
Not then she bids his trembling lips express
The aching gladness, the voluptuous pain.
Life is his poem then; flesh, sense, and brain
One full-stringed lyre attuned to happiness.
But when the dream is done, the pulses fail,
The day's illusion, with the day's sun set,
He, lonely in the twilight, sees the pale
Divine Consoler, featured like Regret,
Enter and clasp his hand and kiss his brow.
Then his lips ope to sing—as mine do now.

## Sympathy

Therefore I dare reveal my private woe,
The secret blots of my imperfect heart,
Nor strive to shrink or swell mine own desert,
Nor beautify nor hide. For this I know,
That even as I am, thou also art.
Thou past heroic forms unmoved shalt go,
To pause and bide with me, to whisper low:
"Not I alone am weak, not I apart
Must suffer, struggle, conquer day by day.
Here is my very cross by strangers borne,
Here is my bosom-sin wherefrom I pray
Hourly deliverance—this my rose, my thorn.
This woman my soul's need can understand,
Stretching o'er silent gulfs her sister hand."


## Youth and Death

What hast thou done to this dear friend of mine,
Thou cold, white, silent Stranger? From my hand
Her clasped hand slips to meet the grasp of thine;
Her eyes that flamed with love, at thy command
Stare stone-blank on blank air; her frozen heart
Forgets my presence. Teach me who thou art,
Vague shadow sliding 'twixt my friend and me.
    I never saw thee till this sudden hour.
What secret door gave entrance unto thee?
    What power is thine, o'ermastering Love's own
        power?

## Age and Death

Come closer, kind, white, long-familiar friend,
　　Embrace me, fold me to thy broad, soft breast.
Life has grown strange and cold, but thou dost bend
　　Mild eyes of blessing wooing to my rest.
So often hast thou come, and from my side
So many hast thou lured, I only bide
Thy beck, to follow glad thy steps divine.
　　Thy world is peopled for me; this world's bare.
　　Through all these years my couch thou didst prepare.
Thou art supreme Love—kiss me—I am thine!


## City Visions

I.

As the blind Milton's memory of light,
The deaf Beethoven's phantasy of tone,
Wrought joys for them surpassing all things known
In our restricted sphere of sound and sight,—
So while the glaring streets of brick and stone
Vex with heat, noise, and dust from morn till night,
I will give rein to Fancy, taking flight
From dismal now and here, and dwell alone
With new-enfranchised senses. All day long,
Think ye 't is I, who sit 'twixt darkened walls,
While ye chase beauty over land and sea?
Uplift on wings of some rare poet's song,
Where the wide billow laughs and leaps and falls,
I soar cloud-high, free as the winds are free.

Who grasps the substance? who 'mid shadows strays?
He who within some dark-bright wood reclines,
'Twixt sleep and waking, where the needled pines
Have cushioned all his couch with soft brown sprays?
He notes not how the living water shines,
Trembling along the cliff, a flickering haze,
Brimming a wine-bright pool, nor lifts his gaze
To read the ancient wonders and the signs.
Does he possess the actual, or do I,
Who paint on air more than his sense receives,
The glittering pine-tufts with closed eyes behold,
Breathe the strong resinous perfume, see the sky
Quiver like azure flame between the leaves,
And open unseen gates with key of gold?

## Influence

The fervent, pale-faced Mother ere she sleep,
Looks out upon the zigzag-lighted square,
The beautiful bare trees, the blue night-air,
The revelation of the star-strewn deep,
World above world, and heaven over heaven.
Between the tree-tops and the skies, her sight
Rests on a steadfast, ruddy-shining light,
High in the tower, and earthly star of even.
Hers is the faith in saints' and angels' power,
And mediating love—she breathes a prayer
For yon tired watcher in the gray old tower.

He the shrewd, skeptic poet unaware
Feels comforted and stilled, and knows not whence
Falls this unwonted peace on heart and sense.

## Restlessness*

Would I had waked this morn where Florence smiles,
A-bloom with beauty, a white rose full-blown,
Yet rich in sacred dust, in storied stone,
Precious past all the wealth of Indian isles—
From olive-hoary Fiesole to feed
On Brunelleschi's dome my hungry eye,
And see against the lotus-colored sky,
Spring the slim belfry graceful as a reed.
To kneel upon the ground where Dante trod,
To breathe the air of immortality
From Angelo and Raphael—*to be*—
Each sense new-quickened by a demi-god.
To hear the liquid Tuscan speech at whiles,
From citizen and peasant, to behold
The heaven of Leonardo washed with gold—
Would I had waked this morn where Florence smiles!

*Written before visiting Florence.

## The New Year

*Rosh-Hashanah, 5643*

Not while the snow-shroud round dead earth is rolled,
   And naked branches point to frozen skies,—
When orchards burn their lamps of fiery gold,
   The grape glows like a jewel, and the corn
A sea of beauty and abundance lies,
         Then the new year is born.

Look where the mother of the months uplifts
   In the green clearness of the unsunned West,
Her ivory horn of plenty, dropping gifts,
   Cool, harvest-feeding dews, fine-winnowed light;
Tired labor with fruition, joy and rest
         Profusely to requite.

Blow, Israel, the sacred cornet! Call
   Back to thy courts whatever faint heart throb
With thine ancestral blood, thy need craves all.
   The red, dark year is dead, the year just born
Leads on from anguish wrought by priest and mob,
         To what undreamed-of morn?

For never yet, since on the holy height,
   The Temple's marble walls of white and green
Carved like the sea-waves, fell, and the world's light
   Went out in darkness,—never was the year
Greater with portent and with promise seen,
         Than this eve now and here.

Even as the Prophet promised, so your tent
    Hath been enlarged unto earth's farthest rim.
To snow-capped Sierras from vast steppes ye went,
    Through fire and blood and tempest-tossing wave,
For freedom to proclaim and worship Him,
                Mighty to slay and save.

High above flood and fire ye held the scroll,
    Out of the depths ye published still the Word.
No bodily pang had power to swerve your soul:
    Ye, in a cynic age of crumbling faiths,
Lived to bear witness to the living Lord,
                Or died a thousand deaths.

In two divided streams the exiles part,
    One rolling homeward to its ancient source,
One rushing sunward with fresh will, new heart.
    By each the truth is spread, the law unfurled,
Each separate soul contains the nation's force,
                And both embrace the world.

Kindle the silver candle's seven rays,
    Offer the first fruits of the clustered bowers,
The garnered spoil of bees. With prayer and praise
    Rejoice that once more tried, once more we prove
How strength of supreme suffering still is ours
                For Truth and Law and Love.

# In Exile

"Since that day till now our life is one unbroken para-
dise. We live a true brotherly life. Every evening after
supper we take a seat under the mighty oak and sing our
songs."—*Extract from a letter of a Russian refugee in Texas.*

Twilight is here, soft breezes bow the grass,
    Day's sounds of various toil break slowly off,
The yoke-freed oxen low, the patient ass
    Dips his dry nostril in the cool, deep trough.
Up from the prairie the tanned herdsmen pass
    With frothy pails, guiding with voices rough
Their udder-lightened kine. Fresh smells of earth,
The rich, black furrows of the glebe send forth.

After the Southern day of heavy toil,
    How good to lie, with limbs relaxed, brows bare
To evening's fan, and watch the smoke-wreaths coil
    Up from one's pipe-stem through the rayless air.
So deem these unused tillers of the soil,
    Who stretched beneath the shadowing oak-tree, stare
Peacefully on the star-unfolding skies,
And name their life unbroken paradise.

The hounded stag that has escaped the pack,
    And pants at ease within a thick-leaved dell;
The unimprisoned bird that finds the track
    Through sun-bathed space, to where his fellows
            dwell;
The martyr, granted respite from the rack,
    The death-doomed victim pardoned from his cell,—

Such only know the joy these exiles gain,—
Life's sharpest rapture is surcease of pain.

Strange faces theirs, wherethrough the Orient sun
    Gleams from the eyes and glows athwart the skin.
Grave lines of studious thought and purpose run
    From curl-crowned forehead to dark-bearded chin.
And over all the seal is stamped thereon
    Of anguish branded by a world of sin,
In fire and blood through ages on their name,
Their seal of glory and the Gentiles' shame.

Freedom to love the law that Moses brought,
    To sing the songs of David, and to think
The thoughts Gabirol to Spinoza taught,
    Freedom to dig the common earth, to drink
The universal air—for this they sought
    Refuge o'er wave and continent, to link
Egypt with Texas in their mystic chain,
And truth's perpetual lamp forbid to wane.

Hark! through the quiet evening air, their song
    Floats forth with wild sweet rhythm and glad refrain.
They sing the conquest of the spirit strong,
    The soul that wrests the victory from pain;
The noble joys of manhood that belong
    To comrades and to brothers. In their strain
Rustle of palms and Eastern streams one hears,
And the broad prairie melts in mist of tears.

# In Memoriam—Rev. J. J. Lyons

*Rosh-Hashanah, 5638*

The golden harvest-tide is here, the corn
Bows its proud tops beneath the reaper's hand.
Ripe orchards' plenteous yields enrich the land;
Bring the first fruits and offer them this morn,
With the stored sweetness of all summer hours,
The amber honey sucked from myriad flowers,
And sacrifice your best first fruits to-day,
With fainting hearts and hands forespent with toil,
Offer the mellow harvest's splendid spoil,
To Him who gives and Him who takes away.

Bring timbrels, bring the harp of sweet accord,
And in a pleasant psalm your voice attune,
And blow the cornet greeting the new moon.
Sing, holy, holy, holy, is the Lord,
Who killeth and who quickeneth again,
Who woundeth, and who healeth mortal pain,
Whose hand afflicts us, and who sends us peace.
Hail thou slim arc of promise in the West,
Thou pledge of certain plenty, peace, and rest.
With the spent year, may the year's sorrows cease.

For there is mourning now in Israel,
The crown, the garland of the branching tree
Is plucked and withered. Ripe of years was he.
The priest, the good old man who wrought so well
Upon his chosen glebe. For he was one
Who at his seed-plot toiled through rain and sun.

Morn found him not as one who slumbereth,
Noon saw him faithful, and the restful night
Stole o'er him at his labors to requite
The just man's service with the just man's death.

What shall be said when such as he do pass?
Go to the hill-side, neath the cypress-trees,
Fall midst that peopled silence on your knees,
And weep that man must wither as the grass.
But mourn him not, whose blameless life complete
Rounded its perfect orb, whose sleep is sweet,
Whom we must follow, but may not recall.
Salute with solemn trumpets the New Year,
And offer honeyed fruits as were he here,
Though ye be sick with wormwood and with gall.

## The Banner of the Jew

Wake, Israel, wake! Recall to-day
   The glorious Maccabean rage,
The sire heroic, hoary-gray,
   His five-fold lion-lineage:
The Wise, the Elect, the Help-of-God,
The Burst-of-Spring, the Avenging Rod.*

From Mizpeh's mountain-ridge they saw
   Jerusalem's empty streets, her shrine

*The sons of Mattathias—Jonathan, John, Eleazar, Simon (also called the Jewel), and Judas, the Prince.

Laid waste where Greeks profaned the Law,
　　With idol and with pagan sign.
Mourners in tattered black were there,
With ashes sprinkled on their hair.

Then from the stony peak there rang
　　A blast to ope the graves: down poured
The Maccabean clan, who sang
　　Their battle-anthem to the Lord.
Five heroes lead, and following, see,
Ten thousand rush to victory!

Oh for Jerusalem's trumpet now,
　　To blow a blast of shattering power,
To wake the sleepers high and low,
　　And rouse them to the urgent hour!
No hand for vengeance—but to save,
A million naked swords should wave.

Oh deem not dead that martial fire,
　　Say not the mystic flame is spent!
With Moses' law and David's lyre,
　　Your ancient strength remains unbent.
Let but an Ezra rise anew,
To lift the *Banner of the Jew!*

A rag, a mock at first—erelong,
　　When men have bled and women wept,
To guard its precious folds from wrong,
　　Even they who shrunk, even they who slept,
Shall leap to bless it, and to save.
Strike! for the brave revere the brave!

## The Guardian of the Red Disk

*Spoken by a Citizen of Malta—1300*

A curious title held in high repute,
One among many honors, thickly strewn
On my lord Bishop's head, his grace of Malta.
Nobly he bears them all,—with tact, skill, zeal,
Fulfills each special office, vast or slight,
Nor slurs the least minutia,—therewithal
Wears such a stately aspect of command,
Broad-cheeked, broad-chested, reverend, sanctified,
Haloed with white about the tonsure's rim,
With dropped lids o'er the piercing Spanish eyes
(Lynx-keen, I warrant, to spy out heresy);
Tall, massive form, o'ertowering all in presence,
Or ere they kneel to kiss the large white hand.
His looks sustain his deeds,—the perfect prelate,
Whose void chair shall be taken, but not filled.
You know not, who are foreign to the isle,
Haply, what this Red Disk may be, he guards.
'T is the bright blotch, big as the Royal seal,
Branded beneath the beard of every Jew.
These vermin so infest the isle, so slide
Into all byways, highways that may lead
Direct or roundabout to wealth or power,
Some plain, plump mark was needed, to protect
From the degrading contact Christian folk.

The evil had grown monstrous: certain Jews
Wore such a haughty air, had so refined,
With super-subtle arts, strict, monkish lives,

And studious habit, the coarse Hebrew type,
One might have elbowed in the public mart
Iscariot,—nor suspected one's soul-peril.
Christ's blood! it sets my flesh a-creep to think!
We may breathe freely now, not fearing taint,
Praised be our good Lord Bishop! He keeps count
Of every Jew, and prints on cheek or chin
The scarlet stamp of separateness, of shame.

No beard, blue-black, grizzled or Judas-colored,
May hide that damning little wafer-flame.
When one appears therewith, the urchins know
Good sport 's at hand; they fling their stones and mud,
Sure of their game. But most the wisdom shows
Upon the unbelievers' selves; they learn
Their proper rank; crouch, cringe, and hide,—lay by
Their insolence of self-esteem; no more
Flaunt forth in rich attire, but in dull weeds,
Slovenly donned, would slink past unobserved;
Bow servile necks and crook obsequious knees,
Chin sunk in hollow chest, eyes fixed on earth
Or blinking sidewise, but to apprehend
Whether or not the hated spot be spied.
I warrant my Lord Bishop has full hands,
Guarding the Red Disk—lest one rogue escape!

# The Valley of Baca

*Psalm LXXXIV*

A brackish lake is there with bitter pools
    Anigh its margin, brushed by heavy trees.
A piping wind the narrow valley cools,
    Fretting the willows and the cypresses.
Gray skies above, and in the gloomy space
An awful presence hath its dwelling-place.

I saw a youth pass down that vale of tears;
    His head was circled with a crown of thorn,
His form was bowed as by the weight of years,
    His wayworn feet by stones were cut and torn.
His eyes were such as have beheld the sword
Of terror of the angel of the Lord.

He passed, and clouds and shadows and thick haze
    Fell and encompassed him. I might not see
What hand upheld him in those dismal ways,
    Wherethrough he staggered with his misery.
The creeping mists that trooped and spread around,
The smitten head and writhing form enwound.

Then slow and gradual but sure they rose,
    Those clinging vapors blotting out the sky.
The youth had fallen not, his viewless foes
    Discomfited, had left the victory
Unto the heart that fainted not nor failed,
But from the hill-tops its salvation hailed.

I looked at him in dread lest I should see,
    The anguish of the struggle in his eyes;
And lo, great peace was there! Triumphantly
    The sunshine crowned him from the sacred skies.
"From strength to strength he goes," he leaves beneath
The valley of the shadow and of death.

"Thrice blest who passing through that vale of Tears,
Makes it a well,"—and draws life-nourishment
From those death-bitter drops. No grief, no fears
    Assail him further, he may scorn the event.
For naught hath power to swerve the steadfast soul
Within that valley broken and made whole.

## The New Ezekiel

What, can these dead bones live, whose sap is dried
    By twenty scorching centuries of wrong?
Is this the House of Israel, whose pride
    Is as a tale that's told, an ancient song?
Are these ignoble relics all that live
    Of psalmist, priest, and prophet? Can the breath
Of very heaven bid these bones revive,
    Open the graves and clothe the ribs of death?

Yea, Prophesy, the Lord hath said. Again
    Say to the wind, Come forth and breathe afresh,
Even that they may live upon these slain,
    And bone to bone shall leap, and flesh to flesh.

The Spirit is not dead, proclaim the word,
　　Where lay dead bones, a host of armed men stand!
I ope your graves, my people, saith the Lord,
　　And I shall place you living in your land.


## Bar Kochba

Weep, Israel! your tardy meed outpour
　　Of grateful homage on his fallen head,
That never coronal of triumph wore,
　　Untombed, dishonored, and unchapleted.
If Victory makes the hero, raw Success
　　The stamp of virtue, unremembered
Be then the desperate strife, the storm and stress
　　Of the last Warrior Jew. But if the man
Who dies for freedom, loving all things less,
　　Against world-legions, mustering his poor clan;
The weak, the wronged, the miserable, to send
　　Their death-cry's protest through the ages' span—
If such an one be worthy, ye shall lend
　　Eternal thanks to him, eternal praise.
Nobler the conquered than the conqueror's end!

## 1492

Thou two-faced year, Mother of Change and Fate,
Didst weep when Spain cast forth with flaming sword,
The children of the prophets of the Lord,
Prince, priest, and people, spurned by zealot hate.
Hounded from sea to sea, from state to state,
The West refused them, and the East abhorred.
No anchorage the known world could afford,
Close-locked was every port, barred every gate.
Then smiling, thou unveil'dst, O two-faced year,
A virgin world where doors of sunset part,
Saying, "Ho, all who weary, enter here!
There falls each ancient barrier that the art
Of race or creed or rank devised, to rear
Grim bulwarked hatred between heart and heart!"

*1883.*


## The Feast of Lights

Kindle the taper like the steadfast star
    Ablaze on evening's forehead o'er the earth,
And add each night a lustre till afar
    An eightfold splendor shine above thy hearth.
Clash, Israel, the cymbals, touch the lyre,
    Blow the brass trumpet and the harsh-tongued horn;
Chant psalms of victory till the heart takes fire,
    The Maccabean spirit leap new-born.

Remember how from wintry dawn till night,
    Such songs were sung in Zion, when again
On the high altar flamed the sacred light,
    And, purified from every Syrian stain,
The foam-white walls with golden shields were hung,
    With crowns and silken spoils, and at the shrine,
Stood, midst their conqueror-tribe, five chieftains
        sprung
    From one heroic stock, one seed divine.

Five branches grown from Mattathias' stem,
    The Blessed John, the Keen-Eyed Jonathan,
Simon the fair, the Burst-of-Spring, the Gem,
    Eleazar, Help-of-God; o'er all his clan
Judas the Lion-Prince, the Avenging Rod,
    Towered in warrior-beauty, uncrowned king,
Armed with the breastplate and the sword of God,
    Whose praise is: "He received the perishing."

They who had camped within the mountain-pass,
    Couched on the rock, and tented neath the sky,
Who saw from Mizpah's heights the tangled grass
    Choke the wide Temple-courts, the altar lie
Disfigured and polluted—who had flung
    Their faces on the stones, and mourned aloud
And rent their garments, wailing with one tongue,
    Crushed as a wind-swept bed of reeds is bowed,

Even they by one voice fired, one heart of flame,
    Though broken reeds, had risen, and were men,
They rushed upon the spoiler and o'ercame,

Each arm for freedom had the strength of ten.
Now is their mourning into dancing turned,
    Their sackcloth doffed for garments of delight,
Week-long the festive torches shall be burned,
    Music and revelry wed day with night.

Still ours the dance, the feast, the glorious Psalm,
    The mystic lights of emblem, and the Word.
Where is our Judas? Where our five-branched palm?
    Where are the lion-warriors of the Lord?
Clash, Israel, the cymbals, touch the lyre,
    Sound the brass trumpet and the harsh-tongued horn,
Chant hymns of victory till the heart take fire,
    The Maccabean spirit leap new-born!

## Gifts

"O World-God, give me Wealth!" the Egyptian cried.
His prayer was granted. High as heaven, behold
Palace and Pyramid; the brimming tide
Of lavish Nile washed all his land with gold.
Armies of slaves toiled ant-wise at his feet,
World-circling traffic roared through mart and street,
His priests were gods, his spice-balmed kings enshrined,
Set death at naught in rock-ribbed charnels deep.
Seek Pharaoh's race to-day and ye shall find
Rust and the moth, silence and dusty sleep.

"O World-God, give me beauty!" cried the Greek.
His prayer was granted. All the earth became
Plastic and vocal to his sense; each peak,
Each grove, each stream, quick with Promethean flame,
Peopled the world with imaged grace and light.
The lyre was his, and his the breathing might
Of the immortal marble, his the play
Of diamond-pointed thought and golden tongue.
Go seek the sun-shine race, ye find to-day
A broken column and a lute unstrung.

"O World-God, give me Power!" the Roman cried.
His prayer was granted. The vast world was chained
A captive to the chariot of his pride.
The blood of myriad provinces was drained
To feed that fierce, insatiable red heart.
Invulnerably bulwarked every part
With serried legions and with close-meshed Code,
Within, the burrowing worm had gnawed its home,
A roofless ruin stands where once abode
The imperial race of everlasting Rome.

"O Godhead, give me Truth!" the Hebrew cried.
His prayer was granted; he became the slave
Of the Idea, a pilgrim far and wide,
Cursed, hated, spurned, and scourged with none to save.
The Pharaohs knew him, and when Greece beheld,
His wisdom wore the hoary crown of Eld.
Beauty he hath forsworn, and wealth and power.
Seek him to-day, and find in every land.
No fire consumes him, neither floods devour;
Immortal through the lamp within his hand.

# By the Waters of Babylon

*Little Poems in Prose*

### I. The Exodus (August 3, 1492.)

1. The Spanish noon is a blaze of azure fire, and the dusty pilgrims crawl like an endless serpent along tree-less plains and bleached high-roads, through rock-split ravines and castellated, cathedral-shadowed towns.

2. The hoary patriarch, wrinkled as an almond shell, bows painfully upon his staff. The beautiful young mother, ivory-pale, well-nigh swoons beneath her burden; in her large enfolding arms nestles her sleeping babe, round her knees flock her little ones with bruised and bleeding feet. "Mother, shall we soon be there?"

3. The youth with Christ-like countenance speaks comfortably to father and brother, to maiden and wife. In his breast, his own heart is broken.

4. The halt, the blind, are amid the train. Sturdy pack-horses laboriously drag the tented wagons wherein lie the sick athirst with fever.

5. The panting mules are urged forward with spur and goad; stuffed are the heavy saddle-bags with the wreckage of ruined homes.

6. Hark to the tinkling silver bells that adorn the tenderly-carried silken scrolls.

7. In the fierce noon-glare a lad bears a kindled lamp; behind its net-work of bronze the airs of heaven breathe not upon its faint purple star.

8. Noble and abject, learned and simple, illustrious and obscure, plod side by side, all brothers now, all merged in one routed army of misfortune.

9. Woe to the straggler who falls by the wayside! no friend shall close his eyes.

10. They leave behind, the grape, the olive, and the fig; the vines they planted, the corn they sowed, the garden-cities of Andalusia and Aragon, Estremadura and La Mancha, of Grenada and Castile; the altar, the hearth, and the grave of their fathers.

11. The townsman spits at their garments, the shepherd quits his flock, the peasant his plow, to pelt with curses and stones; the villager sets on their trail his yelping cur.

12. Oh the weary march, oh the uptorn roots of home, oh the blankness of the receding goal!

13. Listen to their lamentation: *They that ate dainty food are desolate in the streets; they that were reared in scarlet embrace dunghills. They flee away and wander about. Men say among the nations, they shall no more sojourn there; our end is near, our days are full, our doom is come.*

14. Whither shall they turn? for the West hath cast them out, and the East refuseth to receive.

15. O bird of the air, whisper to the despairing exiles, that to-day, to-day, from the many-masted, gayly-bannered port of Palos, sails the world-unveiling Genoese, to unlock the golden gates of sunset and bequeath a Continent to Freedom!


*II. Treasures*

1. Through cycles of darkness the diamond sleeps in its coal-black prison.

2. Purely incrusted in its scaly casket, the breath-tarnished pearl slumbers in mud and ooze.

3. Buried in the bowels of earth, rugged and obscure, lies the ingot of gold.

4. Long hast thou been buried, O Israel, in the bowels of earth; long hast thou slumbered beneath the overwhelming waves; long hast thou slept in the rayless house of darkness.

5. Rejoice and sing, for only thus couldst thou rightly guard the golden knowledge, Truth, the delicate pearl and the adamantine jewel of the Law.

## III. The Sower

1. Over a boundless plain went a man, carrying seed.

2. His face was blackened by sun and rugged from tempest, scarred and distorted by pain. Naked to the loins, his back was ridged with furrows, his breast was plowed with stripes.

3. From his hand dropped the fecund seed.

4. And behold, instantly started from the prepared soil a blade, a sheaf, a springing trunk, a myriad-branching, cloud-aspiring tree. Its arms touched the ends of the horizon, the heavens were darkened with its shadow.

5. It bare blossoms of gold and blossoms of blood, fruitage of health and fruitage of poison; birds sang amid its foliage, and a serpent was coiled about its stem.

6. Under its branches a divinely beautiful man, crowned with thorns, was nailed to a cross.

7. And the tree put forth treacherous boughs to strangle the Sower; his flesh was bruised and torn, but cunningly he disentangled the murderous knot and passed to the eastward.

8. Again there dropped from his hand the fecund seed.

9. And behold, instantly started from the prepared soil a blade, a sheaf, a springing trunk, a myriad-branching, cloud-aspiring tree. Crescent shaped like little emerald moons were the leaves; it bore blossoms of silver and

blossoms of blood, fruitage of health and fruitage of poison; birds sang amid its foliage and a serpent was coiled about its stem.

10. Under its branches a turbaned mighty-limbed Prophet brandished a drawn sword.

11. And behold, this tree likewise puts forth perfidious arms to strangle the Sower; but cunningly he disentangles the murderous knot and passes on.

12. Lo, his hands are not empty of grain, the strength of his arm is not spent.

13. What germ hast thou saved for the future, O miraculous Husbandman? Tell me, thou Planter of Christhood and Islam; tell me, thou seed-bearing Israel!


*IV. The Test*

1. Daylong I brooded upon the Passion of Israel.

2. I saw him bound to the wheel, nailed to the cross, cut off by the sword, burned at the stake, tossed into the seas.

3. And always the patient, resolute, martyr face arose in silent rebuke and defiance.

4. A Prophet with four eyes; wide gazed the orbs of the spirit above the sleeping eyelids of the senses.

5. A Poet, who plucked from his bosom the quivering heart and fashioned it into a lyre.

6. A placid-browed Sage, uplifted from earth in celestial meditation.

7. These I saw, with princes and people in their train; the monumental dead and the standard-bearers of the future.

8. And suddenly I heard a burst of mocking laughter, and turning, I beheld the shuffling gait, the ignominious features, the sordid mask of the son of the Ghetto.

## V. Currents

1. Vast oceanic movements, the flux and reflux of immeasurable tides, oversweep our continent.

2. From the far Caucasian steppes, from the squalid Ghettos of Europe,

3. From Odessa and Bucharest, from Kief, and Ekaterinoslav,

4. Hark to the cry of the exiles of Babylon, the voice of Rachel mourning for her children, of Israel lamenting for Zion.

5. And lo, like a turbid stream, the long-pent flood bursts the dykes of oppression and rushes hitherward.

6. Unto her ample breast, the generous mother of nations welcomes them.

7. The herdsman of Canaan and the seed of Jerusalem's royal shepherd renew their youth amid the pastoral plains of Texas and the golden valleys of the Sierras.


## VI. The Prophet

1. Moses ben Maimon lifting his perpetual lamp over the path of the perplexed;

2. Hallevi, the honey-tongued poet, wakening amid the silent ruins of Zion the sleeping lyre of David;

3. Moses, the wise son of Mendel, who made the Ghetto illustrious;

4. Abarbanel, the counselor of kings; Alcharisi, the exquisite singer; Ibn Ezra, the perfect old man; Gabirol, the tragic seer;

5. Heine, the enchanted magician, the heart-broken jester;

6. Yea, and the century-crowned patriarch whose bounty engirdles the globe;—

7. These need no wreath and no trumpet; like perennial asphodel blossoms, their fame, their glory resounds like the brazen-throated cornet.

8. But thou—hast thou faith in the fortune of Israel? Wouldst thou lighten the anguish of Jacob?

9. Then shalt thou take the hand of yonder caftaned wretch with flowing curls and gold-pierced ears;

10. Who crawls blinking forth from the loathsome recesses of the Jewry;

11. Nerveless his fingers, puny his frame; haunted by the bat-like phantoms of superstition is his brain.

12. Thou shalt say to the bigot, "My Brother," and to the creature of darkness, "My Friend."

13. And thy heart shall spend itself in fountains of love upon the ignorant, the coarse, and the abject.

14. Then in the obscurity thou shalt hear a rush of wings, thine eyes shall be bitten with pungent smoke.

15. And close against thy quivering lips shall be pressed the live coal wherewith the Seraphim brand the Prophets.


*VII. Chrysalis*

1. Long, long has the Orient-Jew spun around his helplessness the cunningly enmeshed web of Talmud and Kabbala.

2. Imprisoned in dark corners of misery and oppression, closely he drew about him the dust-gray filaments, soft as silk and stubborn as steel, until he lay death-stiffened in mummied seclusion.

3. And the world has named him an ugly worm, shunning the blessed daylight.

4. But when the emancipating springtide breathes wholesome, quickening airs, when the Sun of Love shines out with cordial fires, lo, the Soul of Israel bursts her cobweb sheath, and flies forth attired in the winged beauty of immortality.

## Outside the Church

The dark, square belfry tower and massive walls
Fling huge, quaint shadows on the vivid grass;
Through Gothic archways the blue sky is seen;
On the carved stone the generous sunshine falls
With warm, brown tints; athwart the oriel's glass
It casts strange rainbow stains upon the green.

Open the jewelled, pictured windows slant,
That the cool freshness of the soft-sired morn
May enter in; while outward float to me
The deep-voiced organ-chords, the full-choired chant
Above all simple, rural sounds upborne,
And the fine incense' sultry fragrancy.

No grief, no pain those sacred tones express:
Why do they overflow the eyes with tears?
No troublous discord, no pathetic plaint—
They sing the perfect peace of holiness,
Uplift above the reaches of men's fears,
Of grave, great joy and undisturbed content.

The thin, clear echo of the last note dies—
Nay, rather soars beyond our narrow ken
Into a sphere more lofty, vast and wide—

Leaving fulfilled with tears the cheated eyes,
And the foiled heart with longings vague and vain,
Nameless and never to be satisfied.

Where is the utter peace those chants suggest?
Have yonder folk who kneel within at last
Reached its pure source and quaffed the waters calm?
I almost deem that their's is perfect rest,
Disaster, doubt, and evil overpast,
As from without I listen to their psalm.

O Church, to yet one more thy gateways ope,
Who needs all comforts thou canst offer these—
Love, pity, pardon, charity and prayer,
The far-off prospect of a light, a hope
In the fulfilment of life's promises,
A strengthening breath of some diviner air.

O Mother-Church, what solace, what reply,
Hast thou for me? No, I have stood within
The cloistered limitations of thy walls,
With honest efforts, earnest piety,
Imploring refuge from distress and sin,
The grace that on thine own elected falls.

Wearied of those unceasing doubts of mine,
Harassed, perplexed, with one great longing filled:
To hear the mastering word, to yield, adore,
Conquered and happy, crying, "I am thine!
Uplift, sustain, and lead me like a child,
I will repose in thee forevermore."

I waited, but the message did not come;
No voice addressed my reason, and my heart
Shrank to itself in chill discouragement.
To me the ancient oracles were dumb,
The lifeless rites no comfort could impart,
Charged with no answer for my discontent.

Midst blank and stupid faces I could see,
Crowned with strange joy, made beautiful with peace,
Pure brows of women, rapt and fervent-eyed;
And grave men glorying in humility,
Absorbed in quaint and child-like services,
Sincerely moved, devout and satisfied.

The tempered light of many tapers blent
With the stained sunshine; the dim atmosphere,
Dreamy with incense; the organ's rich sea-sound,
Each sense with these was feasted and content.
Neglected still the hungry heart was here,
And no response my mind or spirit found.

Estranged, unsatisfied, I issued forth
(Not there again to look for peace and rest)
Into the broad white light and large sweet air;
And lo! the spring-tide beauty of the earth
Touched tenderly the chord unreached, unguessed,
And all my spirit melted in a prayer.

Here will I seek my peace, here rests my mind,
Knowing "God's comforts are no little thing."
Oh simple souls who yearn with no reply,

Too reverent for religions, ye may find
All patience, all assurance life can bring,
In this free prospect, 'neath this open sky!

Here where I stand, religion seems a part
Of all the moving, teeming, sunlit earth;
All things are sacred, in each bush a God;
No miracles accepts the pious heart,
Where all is miracle; of holy worth
Seems the plain ground our daily feet have trod.

As the majestic choral chant I hear,
The low, impressive organ symphonies,
And with rapt eyes the unfathomed skies I search,
All earth-born troubles wane and disappear,
And I can feel, amidst my reveries,
That not alone I stand outside the church.


## Spring Joy

The wet red glebe shines in the April light,
    The gray hills deepen into green again;
The rainbow hangs in heaven; thin vapors white

Drift o'er the blue, and freckle hill and plain
    With many moving shades; the air is strong
With earth's rich exhalations after rain.

Like a new note breaks forth the ancient song
   Of spring-tide birds, with fresh hope, fresh delight.
Low o'er the fields the marsh-hawk sails along;

Aloft small flocks of pigeons wing their flight;
   Alive with sound and movement is the air;
The short young grass with sunlight rain is bright;

The cherry trees their snow-white garlands wear;
   The garden pranks itself with leaf and flower;
Quick with live seeds the patient earth lies bare.

Oh joy! to see in this expectant hour
   The spirit of life, as on creation's day,
Striving toward perfect form! No fear hath power,

No sense of failure past hath strength to sway
   The immortal hope which swells within the breast,
That this new earth matures not toward decay,

But toward a beauty hitherto unguessed,
   A harvest never dreamed. These mild bright skies,
This lovely uncompleted world, suggest

A powerful joy, a thrill of high surprise,
   Which no fruition ever may inspire,
Albeit each bud should flower, each seed should rise.

## Scenes in the Wood

*(Suggested by Robert Schumann.)*

### I.—*Proem*

The dew-drenched leaves are trembling in the glow
    Of the young morning; thin, clear sunbeams glide
From the low east betwixt black trunks arow,
    To moist cool nooks and pastoral openings wide,
    Flickering on ferns and mosses starry-eyed.
The wet gray grass is lush with dew, and, see!
The filmy meshes sparkle quietly.

The damp dark earth exhales a pungent smell,
    Richer than flowers; a slight translucent haze,
Far down the long bright glades just visible,
    Adds to all gracious forms another grace.
    Anigh us, in this sheltered, shady place,
Upon the freckled ground, incessant move
The quaint brown doubles of the leaves above.

The air is filled with twitter, trill and song,
    And flutter of swift wings from bough and spray;
A frolic breeze the rustling leaves among
    Whispers mysterious joy; the white, new day
    Good tidings brings; the topmost branches sway
'Neath the caressing touches of the morn,
And through the air glad messages are borne.

## II.—Hunting-Song

Wild, lusty-breathing life whose clamor swells
    Upon the breeze, the bark of deep-mouthed hounds,
Harsh horns and clear-keyed bugles, tuneful bells,
    Gallop of clattering hoofs, and rushing sounds
    Of wind-swift motion, echoing to the bounds
Of the dense grove, beyond the leafy lanes,
To far blue uplands over large free plains.

See, where they come, the slim, lithe baying pack,
    With limbs outstretched, wide nostrils, hungry eyes,
Scenting the trail, and, yelling at their back,
    The throng of bright-clad huntsmen, with shrill cries
    Spurring their eager steeds. The whole troop flies,
One breathless moment, past: the echoes wane,
And silence holds the dewy woods again.

## III.—Lonely Flowers

Midmost gnarled roots, brown moss and tangled grass
    Bright sudden flowers! Purple and white and blue,
They prank the green, while, clear and gray as glass,
    Upon their edges shimmers the thin dew.
    They breathe fine subtle odors gently through
The morning air, and gracious thoughts suggest,
And vague strange longings stir within the breast.

These be the very flowers of phantasy,
    That spring from out the common soil of earth,
Moist, living, fragrant, not brought forth to die.
    Surely it is some angel gives them birth,

Who knows their strength, their essence and their
        worth,
And 'mongst the rough roots and the coarse wild weeds
Scatters with generous hand their golden seeds.

Pluck them and taste their honey, crush and smell
    Their bruised-out juice, if thou be bold and strong:
They set the brain afire, their fumes dispel
    Reality and care; fair phantoms throng
    Before the sense with color, light and song;
The forest-shapes grow other than they were,
And blessed spirits people the thin air.

Midst these my master's spirit hovers near,
    The Northern singer, who hath led my feet
To this enchanted ground. Hark! you may hear
    Such strains as Ariel sang, so quaint, so sweet,
    Resounding there where sky and tree-tops meet.
The very echoes of our heart are these—
Our longings, languor, hopes and reveries.

His soul found never vision too sublime,
    Nor image too fantastic, to translate
Into a speech transcending word and rhyme,
    Massive yet supple, weird and delicate.
    Sorrow he maketh beautiful, and Fate.
Within our world he opes a world of dreams
A realm of shadows fed by mystic streams.

## IV.—Haunted Spot

The close-twined branches interlock o'erhead,
    'Twixt leaf and leaf no ray, no glimpse of blue;
From the live roof is gray-green twilight shed,
    Heavily clings at noon the dull chill dew;
    The snake-like roots of the large trees break through
The black, moist sod; rank weeds spread everywhere,
Damp shadow and mirk vapors fill the air.

A yellowish pool hath slowly filtered here
    From drip and ooze and frequent wash of rains:
No lapse of living waters greets the ear,
    Thick crust of slime its sluggish surface stains.
    Here Silence dwells—a vague, wild terror gains
The soul before this mystery divine,
Evil in action, evil in design.

The poisoned flower hath overwrought the brain,
    The wood seems peopled with strange images,
Huge forms uncouth in slow, unending train,
    Life's terrors and its nameless miseries,
    Now like a sullen mist between the trees,
Now close and threatening, distinct and near,
While hateful discords grate upon the ear.

Sin, madness, poverty, disease and age,
    And, halting last, the unmixed evil, death.
How near to her they come, life's heritage
    Of ancient ills! No outlet openeth:
    Her wild cry echoes far above, beneath,
Fills the thick air with trouble, wanes and dies,
Meeting the hollow earth and empty skies.

## V.—*Pleasant Prospect*

Hail, free clear heavens! above our heads again,
　　With white-winged clouds that melt before the sun:
Hail, good green earth! with blossom, grass and grain:
　　O'er the soft rye what silvery ripples run!
　　What tawny shadows! Slowly we have won
This high hill's top: on the wood's edge we stand,
While like a sea below us rolls the land.

The meadows blush with clover, and the air
　　Is honeyed with its keen and spicy smell;
In silence graze the kine, but everywhere
　　Pipe the glad birds that in the forest dwell;
　　Where hearths are set curled wreaths of vapor tell;
Life's grace and promise win the soul again;
Hope floods the heart like sunshine after rain.


## VI.—*Bird as Prophet*

One clear and dainty, softly-fluted note,
　　Then still another, then long, rippling trills
Of joyous music from one warbling throat,
　　Poised in mid-air, that all the woodland fills
　　With reckless rapture, and the grave heart thrills
With answering chords of pleasure, in despite
Of darkness past or swift oncoming night.

We lie with senses tranced as in a dream,
　　Accepting Nature's gladness as our own,
Believing in life's future to redeem

The promise of this hour. O joy unknown!
O love to come! O bursting buds unblown!
Whither may winged song follow you? where find
The substance of those shades that cheat the mind?


### VII.—Night

White stars begin to prick the wan blue sky,
   The trees arise, thick, black and tall; between
Their slim, dark boles gray, film-winged gnats that fly,
   Against the failing western red are seen.
   The footpaths dumb with moss have lost their green.
Mysterious shadows settle everywhere,
A passionate murmur trembles in the air.

Sweet scents wax richer, freshened with cool dews,
   The whole vast forest seems to breathe, to sigh
With rustle, hum and whisper that confuse
   The listening ear, blent with the fitful cry
   Of some belated bird. In the far sky,
Throbbing with stars, there stirs a weird unrest,
Strange joy, akin to pain, fulfills the breast—

A longing born of fears and promises,
   A wild desire, a hope that heeds no bound.
A ray of moonlight struggling through the trees
   Startles us like a phantom; on the ground
   Fall curious shades; white glory spreads around:
The wood is past, and tranquil meadows wide,
Bathed in bright vapor, stretch on every side.

# The Winds

## I.—*South*

Soft from the south the moist wind gently breathes;
O'er the green earth the gray sea-mist is blown,
Thickening the air, blurring with filmy wreaths

The covered face of heaven; it has thrown
Its unstrung beads on the cool, dripping grass;
O'er broad, bright fields, dull seas and low rocks brown,

See how it scours, and rolls a dusky mass
On the effaced horizon, though anigh
'Tis a thin veiled wherethrough the light may pass.

A tender equal radiance fills the sky;
Sweet is the air with smells of early June.
No sun-spot gleams and no deep shadows lie

On the fresh quiet landscape; all atune
In one grave harmony are earth and sea,
And plaintive rainy breeze that tells how soon

Warm showers will follow. This mild wind is he
Painted with cloud-crowned head and floating hair,
Gray beard, gray wings, gray raiment shadowy.

Sad, but yet not as one who hugs despair,
Majestic rather, as who conquers pain,
Into our heart his spirit steals; the air

Kisses the sad brow, soothes the weary brain.
What precious rain is this that blinds the eyes,
While grief dissolves in mist of memories?


### II.—West

Not as of old the harbinger of Spring,
Winging thy noiseless flight through warm soft air,
Pranking the earth with blossoms, scattering

The small bright clouds, and leaving blue skies bare;
The spirit of Autumn unto us art thou,
With weird, wild eyes and streaming, vine-wreathed
  hair.

Ripping gold leaves and brown from branch and bough,
Thou sweepest through late woods, and from the trees,
Still with October's painted flame aglow,

Drawest thine own quaint, lyric harmonies.
Thou sing'st of fruits and harvest; now no more
May the soul nurse her languid reveries.

While mellow fields yield their unstinted store,
Thy breath rebukes her slow activity,
A summons and a challenge, ringing o'er

Wide spaces of free air. Why tarrieth she,
With idle hands, above a mound of clay?
Waken her thou, her inspiration be;

As the dry leaves thou scatterest on thy way,
Her withered fancies, clinging still to death,
Disperse, and chant with her a bolder lay.

Thy voice she heeds, and as she listeneth
Forth from the shadow of the grave she comes,
To large, clear sunshine. Lo! around, beneath,

Like one vast garden, the rich landscape blooms,
With living light afire; the calm stream flows,
Dappled with dusky glories, shifting glooms,

From arching boughs wherethrough the daylight glows,
Like many-tinted wine, and floating leaves
Its crystal fleck with saffron, brown and rose.

O'er earth and air a new, strange spirit weaves
Its subtle spells, for all things melt and fade.
The pomp of burnished woods and golden sheaves

Seems transient as the sunset clouds o'erhead.
Lo, faithless soul! lo, coward sense and dull!
The face of change is also beautiful.

### III.—North

Night, and the vast white fields lie deep with snow.
The high, star-sparkling heavens are bare of cloud,
But northward spectral splendors wax and glow,

Now formless, vague, now a huge crescent bowed,
Crowning with steady light the phantom hills:
Through the stiff trees, that crack with frost, pipes loud

A shrill, sharp wind that all the thin air fills
With piercing music. The Valkyrior,
The fair, fierce spirits, are abroad; those thrills

O'erhead of mystic radiance are no more
Than the cold flash of steel-bright shield and spear,
Flickering above each maiden-warrior.

In the pale sky wild beams shoot far and near,
The wan light spreads, as through a filmy veil
The large, soft, quiet-shining stars appear.

The weird, mysterious glories wane and fail,
The shadowy hosts are noiselessly withdrawn,
And earth lies cold and dumb, awaiting dawn.

### IV.—East

Light March skies dappled with white streaks and flakes,
Dim, faded sunshine like the first faint smile
Of one who after grievous ill awakes

To life and love again. A little while,
And the tranced earth will quicken 'neath the breath
Of mild, reviving airs; now brisk winds pile

Heaped swollen clouds; dull fields lie gray beneath,
And only in warm nooks green blades put forth,
Or a rathe violet shyly blossometh.

This wanton wind is welcome unto earth,
Not for his gifts, but for his promises,
Sure of fulfillment and of priceless worth.

We know what is to come: bright images
Of the world's perfect bloom before us rise,
The hope of those glad hours redeemeth these.

This scant, dry herbage, these chill, clouded skies,
These bare, cold boughs, our fancy leaves behind,
While spring flies forward with the swift-winged wind.


### V.—Calm

Look forth: earth, ocean, air of mid-July
Melt each in other as dream melts in dream,
Glassed in a rosy sea a rosy sky,

Till both one flawless sphere of crystal seem,
Ringed by the dim horizon's purple band.
No cloud above, no ripple and no gleam

To fleck the polished waters; on the land,
Flushed with warm mists, stirreth nor leaf nor blade.
Day-long sweet spicy Southland airs have fanned

The sleepy world; now all at rest are laid.
The far-off, wraith-like vessels, motionless,
Seem hung in nothing, 'twixt the shell o'erhead

And hollow depths below. Soft sounds caress
The listening ear; low insects' drowsy drone,
And feebly-tinkling tide that make no less

The spell of silent calm o'er all things thrown.
The very pulse of Nature seems to cease;
Earth, sea and heaven and windless air breathe peace.


## Phantasmagoria

Last night we sat beside the huge blank sea,
    And from the eastern ridge of shadowy cloud
Watched the big moon swing upward, rolling free
    Through clear star-spaces, till anon a shroud
    Of vaporous film would veil, or some weird crowd
Of shapeless wraiths would blot her light serene
From out the heavens as she had never been.

Flat meadows set with black, gaunt, lonely trees,
    Twisted and bent by many winters' gales,
Stretched landward from the illimitable seas.
    Through their thick leaves the summer's soft breath
        fails,
    Or whispers sleepily fantastic tales:
Wide-rolling waves sang many a mystic rune,
Now vague and vast, now steel-bright 'neath the moon.

Silent we sat, for in the viewless air
    The sacred Mother-Spirit seemed to brood:
Wistful we followed the moon's progress there
    Across the pathless, upper solitude,
    Rejoicing when, in some calm interlude
'Twixt cloud and cloud, she issued bright and pale,
O'er some ethereal lake to slowly sail.

In those mysterious heavens of mid-June,
    Grim dusky dragons oped wide-yawning jaws,
Engulphing that gold fruit which was the moon:
    The growling waves boomed louder in the pause
    Of dim eclipse. Lo! veiled with floating gauze,
Safe she emerged, a bride with radiant eyes,
Lady of love and empress of the skies.

How shall she conquer that terrific shape
    Which crawleth near, and in an instant more
Must leap unswerving? How may she escape?
    Ah! her soft yellow beams pierce to the core
    Of that dread phantom: all her peril's o'er.
In wreaths of silver and in flakes of pearl
The torn cloud-edges round her outline curl.

But brief the respite, for the mists again,
    Close gathering, darken o'er her very face,
And the blind world, bereft, must yearn in vain.
    'Midst the gray floating vapors bides no trace
    Of the late glory streaming from her place:
Slowly the dim procession glides along
As to majestic strains of choired song.

Thus did we watch her fare across the skies,
    Now conquering and now conquered, till at last
In midnight's crystal field her enemies
    Were routed utterly. Her rays were cast
    Unbroken over wide sea-meadows, glassed
In the cool shimmer of the moving tide,
And spread, a web of dreams, on every side.

Rare night of changes, not to be forgot!
    Long did we sit, bound by thy wizard spell,
And tears unshed against our lids pressed hot,
    But quivered not upon the cheek, nor fell,
    The while we watched thy soul made visible,
Now quenched, now kindled. Tranced beneath its beam,
We dreamed again the world-old golden dream.


## Under the Sea

I.

Clear through the shining liquid glass I gazed,
    Discovering a world! There long reeds swung,
Balanced by lazy ripples; sea-plants raised
    Their emerald crowns aloft; dark mosses clung,
Golden and brown, to rocks that seemed fit couch
    For mermaidens and languid water-brides;
Bright tawny bulging sea-weed in its pouch
    Held living jewels twinkling through the sides;
Blue polished pebbles and pink twisted shells
    Paved the clean floor. While my rapt eyes were bent

'Neath the vexed surface, on the crystal cells,
    Through that serene, caressing element,
The tranquil sleep, the eternal rest profound,
I seemed to share of those who have been drowned.


II.

For they are lulled by cradle-song of waves,
    And soft green waters kiss their sealèd eyes;
Round them smooth currents wind through twilight
        caves;
    They sleep on moss, but buried treasure lies
Golden and pearl anigh their crystal graves.
    High overhead they feel the sea-gull dip
With greetings sweet—sighs from some heart that
        craves
    Their drownèd love, kisses from some fond lip,
Whereon the stinging bitterness must dwell
For aye of the unbroken, last farewell.
    But they, possessed by that divine repose,
Stir not, nor give a sign. Shall they awake
Ever from this deep dream? or ever slake
    The thirst for peace life's fevered fret bestows?


## The Christmas Tree

Crusted with silver, gemmed with stars of light,
    Topaz and ruby, emerald, sapphire, pearl,
The enchanted tree within a world of white
Uplifts her myriad crystal branches bright
    Against the pale blue skies. The keen winds whirl

Her globèd jewels on the sheeted snow,
That hard and pure as marble lies below.

Yet even as the radiant fruitage falls,
   Touching the solid earth, it melts to air.
Gold-glimmering rings and clear, flame-hearted balls,—
These be the magic keys to elfin halls.
   The outstretched hands of greed are void and bare,
But elfin hands may clasp, elf eyes may see,
The mystic glories of the wondrous tree.

Lo, as beneath the silver boughs I stood,
   And watched the gleaming jewel in their heart,
Blue as a star, the subtle charm held good:
   I touched and clasped a dropping diamond dart,
   And, rapt from all the snowy world apart,
Alone within the moist, green woods of May,
I wandered ere the middle hour of day.

And over me the magic tree outspread
   Her rustling branches like a silken tent;
An azure light the balmy heavens shed;
Rose-white with odorous bloom above my head,
   Scarce 'neath their burden soft the wreathed sprays
      bent.
Through them went singing birds, and once on high
Surely a blindfold, winged boy-god flew by.

In the cool shade two happy mortals stood
   And laughed, because the spring was in their veins,
Coursing like heavenly fire along their blood,

To see the sunbeams pierce the emerald wood,
   To hear each other's voice, to catch the strains
Of sweet bird-carols in the tree-tops high;
And laughed like gods, who are not born to die.

A spirit murmured in mine ear unseen,
   "Rub well the dart thou holdest." I obeyed,
And all the tree was swathed in living green,
Veiled with hot, hazy sunshine, and between
   The ripe, dark leaves plump cherries white and red,
Swaying on slender stalks with every breeze,
Glowed like the gold fruits of Hesperides.

Once more I rubbed the talisman. There came
   Once more a change: the rusty leaves outshone
With tints of bronze against a sky of flame,
Weird with strange light, the same yet not the same.
   But brief the glory, setting with the sun:
A fog-white wraith uprose to haunt the tree,
And shrill winds whistled through it drearily.

From out my hand the mystic arrow fell:
   Like dew it vanished, and I was aware
Of winter-tide and death. Ah, was it well,
Ye mocking elves, to weave this subtle spell,
   And break it thus, dissolving into air
The fairy fabric of my dream, and show
Life a brief vision melting with the snow?

# The Will-o'-the-Wisp

Between the flat, wide marsh and moonless sky
    Hangs a gray roof of cloud: the rank earth steams.
Hark! far away the sea breaks heavily
    On shelving sands. Is this the world of dreams?
Or can this dun blank, this weird waste, be real?
    See, where a yellow, wavering, thin flame gleams
Yonder above the grass-tips! Watch it steal
    Ghostlike amongst their roots with lambent beams.
Surely it lives! An errant spirit free
    From its clay prison, what delight it owns
In boundless spaces! Lo, I haste to thee,
    Quaint, mystic soul of fire! o'er bog and stones.
Mock me no more, for surely thou art she
    Whose daily loss my widowed heart bemoans.


# Grotesque

*Suggested by a Visit to the Castellani Collection*

All the curious throng has gone;
Eyes audacious, mouths agape,
        Every shape
Of this modern world bizarre.
Whence we come and what we are,
        God or ape,
Each one ponders, grave and wise,
Each one vents a sage surmise
        Of his own.

Oh, the vacant eyes that gaze
Day-long on our helplessness!
      Do they guess
That we, spell-bound images,
Waifs of fairer days than these,
      Dare no less?
As they pass in motley file,
We, too, criticize the while,
      Blame and praise.

For when midnight moonbeams glance
Through the hall, our charm they break.
      We awake,
And we burst our clayey chain,
Breathe and move and live again;
      And we make
All the echoing walls repeat
Noise of stirring tongues and feet,
      Jest and dance.

Come when all the city sleeps.
Phœbus, aureoled with fire,
      Strikes his lyre;
Perseus of the dauntless glance
With yon Roman maid shall dance.
      Drawing nigher,
Cupid's lips and Psyche's meet;
The *Spinario* to his feet,
      Thornless, leaps.

Dionysus wise am I;
All day long serene I stand,
        Mute and bland,
Towering o'er the crowds that press,
Stretching forth, to greet and bless,
        My right hand.
No one offers me a prayer;
The barbarians stop and stare,
        And pass by.


And a sullen ire doth glow
Through these mighty veins of mine,
        Wrath divine.
What new altars do ye feed?
What more godlike gifts succeed
        To the wine;
To the cup of golden mirth
I bestowed on sons of Earth
        Long ago?


Yet when I descend at night,
Living o'er the ancient years
        With my peers,
I must wonder how by day
I could crave from such as they
        Praise or tears.
In these modern hearts of prose
What faith kindles, what love glows,
        What pure light?

To mine ears great names are borne,
Beauty, science, progress, art—
      While apart,
Sappho and Euripides
Calmly hear them prate at ease.
      Sad at heart,
Vainly do I seek a trace
In each sallow, wearied face
      Of earth's morn.

In their service they enlist
Secret currents that have birth
      Under earth,
And their slaves are smoke and air.
Where has beauty fled? and where
      Jocund mirth?
Sunny hope and careless leisure,
Simple joy and natural pleasure,
      They have missed.

Oh, the evil day for me,
When my bed of earth was stirred,
      And I heard
Human voices break my rest,
Joyous cry and flippant jest,
      Spoken word!
And the sunshine smote mine eyes,
With a painful, sharp surprise,
      Suddenly.

Yet, alas! I dreamed but now
That the Ganges near me rolled,
     As of old;
That my worshippers still knelt,
Even as when in shrines I dwelt
     Of red gold.
At my base a poet stood;
Love and longing fired his blood,
     Lit his brow;

And I knew his heart was mine;
And I felt that Circumstance,
     Time, and Chance
Are but shadows; still the same,
Leaps the soul of youth like flame,
     At a glance
Knowing, worshipping the god
Of the joy-inspiring rod
     And the vine.

## The Taming of the Falcon

The bird sits spelled upon the lithe brown wrist
  Of yonder turbaned fowler, who hath lamed
  No feathered limb, but the winged spirit tamed
With his compelling eye. He need not twist
The silken toil, nor set the thick-limed snare;
  He lures the wanderer with his steadfast gaze,
  It shrinks, it quails, it trembles—yet obeys,

And lo! he has enslaved the thing of air.
The fixed, insistent human will is lord
   Of all the earth;—but in the awful sky,
Reigns absolute, unreached by deed or word,
   Above creation, through eternity,
Outshining the sun's shield, the lightning's sword,
   The might of Allah's unaverted eye.


## Progress and Poverty

*(After Reading Mr. Henry George's Book.)*


Oh splendid age when Science lights her lamp
At the brief lightning's momentary flame,
Fixing it steadfast as a star, man's name
Upon the very brow of heaven to stamp!
Launched on a ship whose iron-cuirassed sides
Mock storm and wave, Humanity sails free;
Gayly upon a vast, untraveled sea,
O'er pathless wastes, to ports undreamed she rides,
Richer than Cleopatra's barge of gold,
This vessel, manned by demi-gods, with freight
Of priceless marvels. But where yawns the hold
In that deep, reeking hell, what slaves be they,
Who feed the ravenous monster, pant and sweat,
Nor know if overhead reign night or day?

## To R.W.E.

As, when a father dies, his children draw
About the empty hearth, their loss to cheat
With uttered praise and love, and oft repeat
His all-familiar words with whispered awe,—
The honored habit of his daily law;
Not for his sake, but theirs, whose feebler feet
Need still that guiding lamp, whose faith less sweet
Misses that tempered patience without flaw;—
So do we gather round thy vacant chair,
In thine own elm-roofed, amber-rivered town,
Master and father! For the love we bear,
Not for thy fame's sake, do we weave this crown,
And feel thy presence in the sacred air,
Forbidding us to weep that thou art gone.

*New York, May, 1884.*


## Assurance

Last night I slept, & when I woke her kiss
Still floated on my lips. For we had strayed
Together in my dream, through some dim glade,
Where the shy moonbeams scarce dared light our bliss.
The air was dank with dew, between the trees,
The hidden glow-worms kindled & were spent.
Cheek pressed to cheek, the cool, the hot night-breeze
Mingled our hair, our breath, & came & went,

As sporting with our passion. Low & deep,
Spake in mine ear her voice:

                              "And didst thou dream,
This could be buried? this could be asleep?
And love be thrall to death? Nay, whatso seem,
Have faith, dear heart; *this is the thing that is!*"
Thereon I woke, and on my lips her kiss.

## Donna Clara

In the evening through her garden
Wanders the Alcalde's daughter;
Festal sounds of drum and trumpet
Ring out hither from the castle.

"I am weary of the dances,
Honeyed words of adulation
From the knights who still compare me
To the sun,—with dainty phrases.

"Yes, of all things I am weary,
Since I first beheld by moonlight,
Him my cavalier, whose zither
Nightly draws me to my casement.

"As he stands, so slim and daring,
With his flaming eyes that sparkle
From his nobly-pallid features,
Truly he St. George resembles."

Thus went Donna Clara dreaming,
On the ground her eyes were fastened,
When she raised them, lo! before her
Stood the handsome, knightly stranger.

Pressing hands and whispering passion,
These twain wander in the moonlight.
Gently doth the breeze caress them,
The enchanted roses greet them.

The enchanted roses greet them,
 And they glow like love's own heralds;
"Tell me, tell me, my belovèd,
Wherefore, all at once thou blushest."

"Gnats were stinging me, my darling,
And I hate these gnats in summer,
E'en as though they were a rabble
Of vile Jews with long, hooked noses."

"Heed not gnats nor Jews, belovèd,"
Spake the knight with fond endearments.
From the almond-tree dropped downward
Myriad snowy flakes of blossoms.

Myriad snowy flakes of blossoms
Shed around them fragrant odors.
"Tell me, tell me, my belovèd,
Looks thy heart on me with favor?"

"Yes, I love thee, oh my darling,
And I swear it by our Savior,
Whom the accursèd Jews did murder
Long ago with wicked malice."

"Heed thou neither Jews nor Savior,"
Spake the knight with fond endearments;
Far-off waved as in a vision
Gleaming lilies bathed in moonlight.

Gleaming lilies bathed in moonlight
Seemed to watch the stars above them.
"Tell me, tell me, my belovèd,
Didst thou not erewhile swear falsely?"

"Naught is false in me, my darling,
E'en as in my bosom floweth
Not a drop of blood that's Moorish,
Neither of foul Jewish current."

"Heed not Moors nor Jews, belovèd,"
Spake the knight with fond endearments.
Then towards a grove of myrtles
Leads he the Alcalde's daughter.

And with love's slight, subtle meshes,
He hath trapped her and entangled;
Brief their words, but long their kisses,
For their hearts are overflowing.

What a melting bridal carol,
Sings the nightingale, the pure one!
How the fire-flies in the grasses
Trip their sparkling, torch-light dances!

In the grove the silence deepens;
Naught is heard save furtive rustling
Of the swaying myrtle branches,
And the breathing of the flowers.

But the sound of drum and trumpet
Burst forth sudden from the castle.
Rudely they awaken Clara,
Pillowed on her lover's bosom.

"Hark, they summon me, my darling.
But before I go, oh tell me,
Tell me what thy precious name is,
Which so closely thou hast hidden."

And the knight, with gentle laughter,
Kissed the fingers of his donna,
Kissed her lips and kissed her forehead,
And at last these words he uttered:

"I, Señora, your belovèd,
Am the son of the respected
Worthy, erudite Grand Rabbi,
Israel of Saragossa!"

*Heine*

## Song

There stands a lonely pine-tree
    In the north, on a barren height;
He sleeps while the ice and snow flakes
    Swathe him in folds of white.

He dreameth of a palm-tree
    Far in the sunrise-land,
Lonely and silent longing
    On her burning bank of sand.

*Heine*


FROM **The North Sea, First Cyclus**

*II. Twilight*

    On the wan shore of the sea
    Lonely I sat with troubled thoughts.
    The sun dropped lower, and cast
    Glowing red streaks on the water.
    And the white wide waves,
    Crowding in with the tide,
    Foamed and rustled, nearer and nearer,
With a strange rustling, a whispering, a hissing,
A laughter, a murmur, a sighing, a seething,
And amidst all these a mysterious lullaby.
    I seemed to hear long-past traditions,
    Lovely old-time fairy-tales,

Which as a boy I had heard,
From the neighbor's children,
When on summer evenings we had nestled
On the stone steps of the porch.
With little eager hearts,
And wistful cunning eyes,
Whilst the grown maidens
Sat opposite at their windows
Near their sweet-smelling flower pots,
With their rosy faces,
Smiling and beaming in the moonlight.

*Heine*

## Night-Piece

Night, and the heavens beam serene with peace,
Like a pure heart benignly smiles the moon.
Oh, guard thy blessed beauty from mischance,
This I beseech thee in all tender love.
See where the Storm his cloudy mantle spreads,
An ashy curtain covereth the moon.
As if the tempest thirsted for the rain,
The clouds he presses, till they burst in streams.

Heaven wears a dusky raiment, and the moon
Appeareth dead—her tomb is yonder cloud,
And weeping shades come after, like the people
Who mourn with tearful grief a noble queen.

But look! the thunder pierced night's close-linked mail,
His keen-tipped lance of lightning brandishing;
He hovers like a seraph-conqueror.—
Dazed by the flaming splendor of his wings,
In rapid flight as in a whirling dance,
The black cloud-ravens hurry scared away.
So, though the powers of darkness chain my soul,
My heart, a hero, chafes and breaks its bonds.

*Ibn Gabirol*


FROM **On the Voyage to Jerusalem**


*To the West Wind*

O West, how fragrant breathes thy gentle air,
Spikenard and aloes on thy pinions glide.
Thou blow'st from spicy chambers, not from there
Where angry winds and tempests fierce abide.
As on a bird's wings thou dost waft me home,
Sweet as a bundle of rich myrrh to me.
And after thee yearn all the throngs that roam
And furrow with light keel the rolling sea.
Desert her not—our ship—bide with her oft,
When the day sinks and in the morning light.
Smooth thou the deeps and make the billows soft,
Nor rest save at our goal, the sacred height.
Chide thou the East that chafes the raging flood,
And swells the towering surges wild and rude.
What can I do, the elements' poor slave?

Now do they hold me fast, now leave me free;
Cling to the Lord, my soul, for He will save,
Who caused the mountains and the winds to be.

*Judah ha-Levi*


## From the Book of Tarshish, or "Necklace of Pearls"

I.

The shadow of the houses leave behind,
In the cool boscage of the grove reclined,
The wine of friendship from love's goblet drink,
And entertain with cheerful speech the mind.

Drink, friend! behold, the dreary winter's gone,
The mantle of old age has time withdrawn.
The sunbeam glitters in the morning dew,
O'er hill and vale youth's bloom is surging on.

Cup-bearer! quench with snow the goblet's fire,
Even as the wise man cools and stills his ire.
Look, when the jar is drained, upon the brim
The light foam melteth with the heart's desire.

Cup-bearer! bring anear the silver bowl,
And with the glowing gold fulfil the whole,
Unto the weak new vigor it imparts,
And without lance subdues the hero's soul.

My love sways, dancing, like the myrtle-tree,
The masses of her curls disheveled, see!
She kills me with her darts, intoxicates
My burning blood, and will not set me free.

Within the aromatic garden come,
And slowly in its shadows let us roam,
The foliage be the turban for our brows,
And the green branches o'er our heads a dome.

All pain thou with the goblet shalt assuage,
The wine-cup heals the sharpest pangs that rage,
Let others crave inheritance of wealth,
Joy be our portion and our heritage.

Drink in the garden, friend, anigh the rose,
Richer than spice's breath the soft air blows,
If it should cease a little traitor then,
A zephyr light its secret would disclose.

*Ibn Ezra*

# BIOGRAPHICAL NOTE

Emma Lazarus was born on July 22, 1849, in New York City. She was the daughter of Esther Nathan, of German-Jewish descent, and Moses Lazarus, a wealthy sugar merchant from a Sephardic family that had lived in America since at least the eighteenth century. She was educated by private tutors and learned German, French, and Italian at an early age. She received little religious instruction as a child. *Poems and Translations*, printed in 1866 at her father's expense, was brought out in expanded form by a New York publisher in 1867. Lazarus published *Admetus and Other Poems* (1871); the historical novel *Alide: An Episode in Goethe's Life* (1874); *The Spagnoletto* (1876), a verse drama about the seventeenth-century painter Jose de Ribera; and the volume of translations *Poems and Ballads of Heinrich Heine* (1881). She also translated (from German versions) medieval Hebrew poetry. Her poems frequently appeared in *Lippincott's*, *Scribner's*, *The Galaxy*, *The Century*, and other leading periodicals. Outraged by Russian pogroms of the early 1880s, and deeply impressed by a visit to the immigration center at Ward's Island in 1881, Lazarus became a prominent worker for Jewish causes, organizing refugee relief and contributing articles on Jewish subjects to *The Century* as well as writing the weekly column "An Epistle to the Hebrews" for *The American Hebrew*, 1882–83. In 1882 she published *Songs of a Semite*, which included "The Dance to Death," a verse drama about a fourteenth-century massacre of German Jews. Her sonnet "The New Colossus" was written in support of a fundraising campaign to build a pedestal for the Statue of Liberty in New York harbor; the poem was recited in 1886 at the statue's dedication and its final lines were later embossed on the pedestal. She traveled to England and France in 1883, where she met Robert Browning and William Morris. Ill with cancer, she made a long trip to Europe from 1885 to 1887, visiting the Netherlands, France, and Italy. She died on November 19, 1887. A posthumous two-volume edition of her works, *The Poems of Emma Lazarus*, edited by her sisters Mary and Annie, was published in 1889.

## NOTE ON THE TEXTS

In the present volume, the texts of "Niagara" and "Niagara River Below the Falls" are taken from Emma Lazarus' first book, *Poems and Translations* (New York: Hurd and Houghton, 1867). The source for the poems from "Niagara" to "The Day of Dead Soldiers" is *Admetus and Other Poems* (New York: Hurd and Houghton, 1871). The texts of the poems from "Epochs" to "By the Waters of Babylon," along with the translations of medieval Hebrew poets ("Night-Piece," "To the West Wind" from "On the Voyage to Jerusalem," and "From the Book of Tarshish, or 'Necklace of Pearls'") are taken from *Poems* (Boston: Houghton, Mifflin & Co.,1889), the two-volume post-humous gathering of Lazarus' poems edited by her sisters. Several poems from *Poems and Translations* and *Admetus and Other Poems* were included in this edition; the present volume groups these with *Poems* rather than the books in which they were first published because the texts printed here are taken from *Poems*.

The texts in the "Uncollected Poems" section are printed from the following publications:

Outside the Church. *The Index*, December 14, 1872.
Spring Joy. *Lippincott's Magazine*, May 1875.
Scenes in the Wood. *Lippincott's Magazine*, August 1875.

The Winds. *Lippincott's Magazine*, October 1875.

Phantasmagoria. *Lippincott's Magazine*, August 1876.

Under the Sea. *Lippincott's Magazine*, October 1876.

The Christmas Tree. *Lippincott's Magazine*, February 1877.

The Will-o'-the-Wisp. *Lippincott's Magazine*, April 1877.

Grotesque. *The Galaxy*, December 1877.

The Taming of the Falcon. William Sharp (ed.), *American Sonnets* (New York: W. J. Gage & Co., 1889).

Progress and Poverty. *New York Times*, October 2, 1881.

To R.W.E. *Concord School of Philosophy* (Boston: Kennikat Press, 1885).

Assurance. Manuscript Notebook of Poetry, Emma Lazarus Papers, American Jewish Historical Society, Waltham Mass., and New York. This poem was not published in Lazarus' lifetime.

The source for Lazarus' three Heine translations printed here is *Poems and Ballads of Heinrich Heine* (New York: R. Worthington, 1881).

This volume presents the texts of the original printings chosen for inclusion here, but it does not attempt to reproduce nontextual features of their typographic design. The texts are presented without change, except for the correction of typographical errors. Spelling, punctuation, and capitalization are often expressive features and are not altered, even when inconsistent or irregular. The following typographical errors have been corrected (cited by page and line number): 88.12, Burst-of Spring; 88.13, Help of-God; 93.32, bare.

# NOTES

9.1     Jewish Synagogue] The Touro Synagogue, dedicated in 1763 and designed by architect Peter Harrison. This poem is a response to Longfellow's poem, "The Jewish Cemetery at Newport."

9.8     "perpetual lamp"] The lamp always kept alight in synagogues.

9.18    patriarch] Abraham.

9.22    sky-kissed mount] Mt. Sinai, where Moses received the Tables of the Law.

10.4    exiles . . . Babylon] Cf. Psalm 137:1: "By the rivers of Babylon, there we sat down, yea, we wept, when we remembered Zion."

13.1    The Garden of Adonis] An earthly paradise in Book III, Canto VI of *The Faerie Queene*, where "There is continuall spring, and harvest there / Continuall, both meeting at one tyme." "Change" is not found in Spenser's garden.

17.17   central mount of Maine] Mt. Katahdin (elev. 5267). Its name in Abenaki means "principal mountain."

18.11   Sabbath-day] Decoration Day (now Memorial Day) had been established in 1868; in 1869 it fell on a Sunday.

20.5–6  *"The epochs . . . walk."*] From Emerson's "Spiritual Laws" in *Essays, First Series* (1841).

23.7    distant isle] England, here seen as too long the ruler of American poetry.

28.2    *After Robert Schumann*] Specifically Schumann's *Fantasiestücke* for piano, op. 12 (originally titled *"Phantasien"*). The section titles of Lazarus' poem are translations of the eight titles of Schumann's suite: *Des*

143

*Abends*; *Aufschwung*; *Warum?*; *Grillen*; *In der Nacht*; *Fabel*; *Traumswirren*; *Ende vom Lied*.

37.12    *Vega*]    Fertile plain.

38.1    Lindaraxa's bower]    The 16th-century Jardin de Lindaraja, named for Lindaraxa, daughter of an Alcayde of Málaga, fabled for her beauty.

39.3–6    "The Last Sigh" . . . good-by]    Boabdil (Abu Abdullah), the last Moorish ruler of Granada, surrendered the city in January 1492 to Ferdinand and Isabella of Spain. The high point from which he regarded Granada for the last time is known as *"El Ultimo Sospiro del Moro"* ("The Moor's Last Sigh").

39.19    Rough Point]    A rocky promontory in Newport, Rhode Island.

43.6    Undine]    A water-spirit, in Friedrich de la Motte Fouqué's novel *Undine* (1811).

45.15    anana]    Pineapple; the plant it grows on is not in fact a tree.

50.17    *Willis*]    Spirits of dead unwed maidens who take vengeance on young men by dancing them to death, from a story by Heinrich Heine (adapted from Slavic legend) and, subsequently, the celebrated ballet *Giselle* (1840).

51.24    Baldur]    Norse god of light, son of Odin, called "the beautiful" and "the slain god." His death heralds the coming of *Ragnarok*, the apocalyptic conflagration in which nearly all the Norse gods perish.

51.26    'Universal Pan is dead!']    In *Moralia*, Plutarch recounts a legend that in the reign of Tiberius an Egyptian pilot on a ship sailing from Greece toward Italy heard the cry "The great god Pan is dead," and was told to tell the news at the port of Palodes. When he did, his announcement was met with wailing and lamentation. Later Christian commentators said that the pilot heard the cry at the moment of the Crucifixion, and that it signified the cessation of all pagan oracles.

51.27    *Requiescant!*]    "Let them rest."

59.1    Venus of the Louvre]    The Venus de Milo.

59.12    Here *Heine* wept!]    During the terrible decade of pain and illness that he called his "mattress-grave," Heine visited the Venus de Milo in the Louvre. As Lazarus' sister wrote in the Introduction to *Poems*, "She, too, the last time she went out, dragged herself to the Louvre, to the feet of the Venus, 'the goddess without arms who could not help.'" (The last phrase a quote from Heine about his own painful visit of veneration.)

61.22    Symphonic Studies]    Schumann's *Symphonische Etuden*, op. 13, consists of one theme followed by 12 études.

63.22    goddess]    Venus.

66.17    *1856*]   Year of the birth of Napoleon Eugene, Prince Imperial, son of Napoleon III.

67.6    *1879*]   Year of Napoleon Eugene's death while serving with the British Army in Zululand (in present-day South Africa) in the Anglo-Zulu War.

67.17–19    Don Carlos . . . Dauphin]   Don Carlos (1545–68), son of Philip II of Spain, died after much ill-treatment in prison; Arthur of Brittany (1187–1203), grandson of Henry II of England, was murdered by order of his uncle, King John; Louis-Charles, heir to the throne of deposed French king Louis XVI (1785–95), died, also ill-treated, in prison.

68.10    The Cranes of Ibycus]   According to legend, the Greek lyric poet Ibycus (6th cent. B.C.E.), as he was murdered by robbers in a deserted place, called on cranes flying overhead to avenge him. Long afterward, one of the robbers, seeing some cranes, called out to one of his fellows, "Look! Ibycus's avengers," thus revealing their guilt.

69.1    Critic and Poet]   The critic is Matthew Arnold, whose lecture on Emerson Lazarus heard in January 1884. The epigraph to this poem alters Arnold's words: "Milton says that poetry must be simple, sensuous and impassioned. Well, Emerson's poetry is seldom either simple or sensuous or impassioned." (Milton's phrase from *Of Education* is actually "simple, sensuous and passionate.")

69.20    St. Michael's Chapel]   In Canterbury Cathedral.

70.7    A lady]   Lady Margaret Holland, flanked by her two predeceased husbands.

75.2    *5643*]   Corresponding to 1882.

76.21–22    first fruits . . . bees]   The holiday is traditionally celebrated by dipping apples into honey.

78.13    Gabirol]   Solomon Ibn Gabirol (c.1022–70), Hebrew poet and philosopher of medieval Spain, and an influence on Spinoza.

79.1    J. J. Lyons]   Jacques Judah Lyons (1813–77), Lazarus' uncle, a cantor, and rabbi (1839–77) of the Congregation Shearith Israel in New York City; he was a historian of Jewish life in the Western Hemisphere.

79.2    *5638*]   Corresponds to 1877.

79.15    cornet]   The *shofar*, a ram's horn blown in synagogues at the New Year (the timbrels and harp are instruments frequently invoked in the Psalms).

80.17    Maccabean]   In the second century B.C.E. Antiochus IV captured Jerusalem and dedicated the Temple to Zeus. Judas Maccabeus and his brothers led a revolt that overthrew Antiochus' rule and rededicated the Temple. This is celebrated by Jews in the festival of Chanukah.

80.22    Mizpeh] Hill near Jerusalem (alternate spelling, "Mizpah").

82.1    Red Disk] From the early 13th through the 18th centuries, Jews in many parts of Europe were compelled to wear identifying badges of various colors and shapes.

83.9    Judas-colored] Bright red (from medieval representations of Judas Iscariot with red hair and beard).

84.1    Baca] A dry place on the road to Jerusalem.

84.9    vale of tears] Lazarus plays on an etymology of the Hebrew word *baca* meaning "weeping," but she may have known that the Latin Vulgate translates this phrase "*valle lacrymarum.*"

85.5    "From strength . . . goes,"] Cf. Psalm 84:7.

85.7–8    "Thrice blest . . . well,"] Cf. Psalm 84:5–6.

85.14    can these . . . live] Cf. Ezekiel 37:3: "Son of man, can these bones live?"

85.22    Yea, Prophesy . . . said] Ezekiel 37:4.

86.5    Bar Kochba] Simeon Bar Koseva, fierce leader of a revolt against Rome, 132–35 C.E., was killed in battle and his army defeated.

87.17    The Feast of Lights] Chanukah.

89.24    Rust and the moth] "Lay not up for yourselves treasures upon earth, where moth and rust doth corrupt": Matthew 6:19.

91.3    *August 3, 1492*] The day Columbus sailed westward and the day after the expulsion of the Jews from Spain.

91.24    scrolls] The scrolls of the Torah, the five books of Moses; in synagogues, they are covered with rich cloth and adorned with silver ornaments.

91.25    kindled lamp] See note 9.8.

92.14–16    *They that ate . . . dunghills*] Lamentations 4:5.

92.23    Palos] Port in Spain from which Columbus embarked.

95.6–7    Odessa . . . Ekaterinoslav] Cities in which major pogroms occurred in the early 1880s.

96. 21    live coal] See Isaiah 6:6–7.

103.2    *Suggested . . . Schumann*] Specifically Schumann's *Waldszenen*, op. 82; most of the poem's section titles correspond to those of Schumann's composition. The *Waldszenen* is divided into nine parts: *Eintritt* (Introduction); *Jäger auf der Lauer* (Hunter in Ambush); *Einsame Blumen* (Lonely Flowers); *Verrufene Stelle* (Haunted Spot); *Freundliche Landschaft* (Pleasant Landscape); *Herberge* (Shelter); *Vogel als Prophet* (Bird as Prophet); *Jagdlied* (Hunting-Song); *Abschied* (Farewell).

120.17    *Castellani Collection*] After being displayed at the Centennial Exposition in Philadelphia in 1876, the collection of the Italian jewelers Alessandro and Augusto Castellani, consisting of sculpture, ivories, gems, and majolica, was exhibited at the Metropolitan Museum of Art early in 1877.

121.26    *Spinario*]    A celebrated Hellenistic bronze of a boy pulling a thorn from his foot; a stone copy, now in the British Museum, was once part of the Castellani Collection.

125.8    Progress and Poverty]    Economic treatise (1879) by Henry George.

126.1    R.W.E.]    Ralph Waldo Emerson.

128.2    Donna Clara]    This translation from Heine and those that follow are from his *Buch der Lieder* (1837).

132.1    Song]    "*Ein Fichtenbaum steht einsam*" from the poetic sequence "*Lyrisches Intermezzo.*"

133.12    Night-Piece]    This translation consists of two fragments of a longer poem by Gabirol (beginning "*ani ha-ish* . . .") about a storm at night. This and the next two translations were done from German versions of the Hebrew.

134.11    *West Wind*]    A translation of Judah ha-Levi's *zeh ruach, tsad ma'arav* ("This wind, O, West . . .").

135.5    Book of Tarshish]    The Hebrew title is *Sefer ha-anak*, a long poem of many parts.

# INDEX OF TITLES
# AND FIRST LINES

# AMERICAN POETS PROJECT